PRACTICAL HORARY ASTROLOGY

Practical Horary Astrology

GAYATRI DEVI VASUDEV

MOTILAL BANARSIDASS
INTERNATIONAL
DELHI

Reprint Edition : Delhi, 2025
Fourth Edition : 1992

© MOTILAL BANARSIDASS INTERNATIONAL
All Rights Reserved

ISBN : 978-93-48128-97-3 (PB)
ISBN : 978-93-48128-58-4 (HB)

Also available at
MOTILAL BANARSIDASS INTERNATIONAL
H.O. : 41 U.A. Bungalow Road, (Back Lane)Jawahar Nagar, Delhi - 110 007
4261 (basement) Lane #3,Ansari Road, Darya Ganj, New Delhi - 110 002
Shop No. 6, Luz Ginza Complex, 241 Luz Corner, Mylapore, Chennai - 600 004
12/1A, 2nd Floor, Bankim Chatterjee Street, Kolkata - 700 073
Stockist : Motilal Books, Ashok Rajpath, Near Kali Mandir, Patna - 800 004

No part of this book may be reproduced in any form or by any electronic
or mechanical means including information storage and retrieval systems
without permission in writing from the publishers, excepts by a reviewer
who may quote brief passages in a review.

Printed in India
MOTILAL BANARSIDASS INTERNATIONAL

Foreword

It gives me great pleasure to write a few words by way of Foreword to Practical Horary Astrology. The author Gayatri Devi Raman is my daughter. She has made an intelligent study of both natal and horary astrology and has gained considerable experience as a correct predictor on the basis of horary charts. She has already made her mark as a feature-writer in The Astrological Magazine.

Horary astrology is, perhaps, the most important aspect of predictive astrology, where the data employed are accurate and verification of predicted events is possible quickly. In fact, horary is more useful than natal, because it caters to important problems met with in the daily life of the average man and woman.

This book has been done by my daughter with skill and ability. She has dealt with the subject clearly and convincingly in a simple and easily understandable style. The illustrations given are all drawn from the charts handled by her.

The need for such a book, dealing with horary astrology in a practical and non-technical manner, has been long felt. I am happy that my daughter has supplied this want.

The book will be found to be useful not only to the beginner with the merest acquaintance with astrology but also to the advanced student and the professional astrologer.

My daughter tends to hold her own in the future and I hope more books will be coming out of her pen on aspects of astrology not so far touched by me.

Blessing her with all my heart and wishing her a long and fruitful life of service to the public.

29.3.1979   **B.V. Raman**

Preface

In no venue of life is horary astrology more applicable and useful than in daily life. Yet, this branch of astrology has not been fully explored. There have been many translations of classical works on the subject but no real text-book on the art of answering horary questions.

I found most classical works contained definite planetary combinations indicative of definite answers to queries. But these planetary combinations occurred ever so rarely in actuality that I was forced to look for more practical planetary positions that could help us find answers. I discovered that most of horary astrology could be boiled down to a few basic principles. These principles could be extended to apply to any planetary juxtaposition obtaining at the moment of the question.

I began the study of horary astrology with an English translation of Neelakanta's **Prasna Tantra** by my father Dr. B.V. Raman, next took up the translations of Bhattotpala's **Prasnagnana** and **Shatpanchasika** by the late Sri. V. Subramanya Sastri, then the rare Kerala classic **Prasna Marga** (Chapters 1 to 16) while it was in the process of being translated and revised by my father and finally came back to **Prasna Tantra.** Studying it over and over again, I pitched upon a fundamental principle that could answer any question. This principle, I found, lay in Ithasala Yoga, a combination of two planets in a particular way. Other Yogas such as Easarapha, Komboola, Nakta, Radda etc., where but extensions and qualifications of this Yoga.

My father Dr. B.V. Raman has been my Guru in astrology. I have had the rare privilege of spending all my life so far with my Guru. These years have been filled with astrological discussions on almost everything on earth ranging from the colour of one's dress to Marxism to Sankhya philosophy to marriage to success to death and even after life. These discussions have given me rare insights into the science of astrology which no book can offer. But what I have learnt can fill many books.

My mother Smt. Rajeswari Raman has also indirectly played the role of a Guru when she plied me with questions on just about everything under the sun. Trying to answer them was an exercise in horary planetary gymnastics which tested my interpretative ability.

I have sought to fill these pages with what I have learnt under my Guru and from my own experience of handling a wide range of cases.

A basic understanding of general astrology which includes casting the horoscope is necessary for a study of this book. If the principles outlined here are applied diligently, it should be quite easy to answer most questions. I trust all those genuinely interested in discovering truth will find this book useful.

I thank Mr. J.P. Jain and Mr. Abhishek Jain of Motilal Banarasidass International, who have always supported our work in astrology right from the time of my revered father, the late Dr. B.V. Raman, for publishing the book elegantly.

Bangalore **Gayatri Devi Vasudev**
September 2024

Preface to the Fourth Edition

Horary astrology is one of the simpler topics in astrology and highly popular since it purports to matters of immediate or urgent interest to the querent.

The third edition of this book has been extremely well-received by the interested public. Hence, the fourth edition in a short time thereafter.

I am greatful to the Publisher for bringing out this edition in the shortest possible time.

"Sri Rajeswari" **Gayatri Devi Vasudev**
Bangalore – 560 020
1st February, 1992

Preface to the First Edition

In no venue of life is horary astrology more applicable and useful than in daily life. Yet, this branch of astrology has not been fully explored. There have been many translations of classical works on the subject but no real text-book on the art of answering horary questions.

I found most classical works contained definite planetary combinations indicative of definite answers to queries. But these planetary combinations occurred ever so rarely in actually that I was forced to look for more practical planetary positions that could help us find ansers. I discovered that most of horary astrology could boiled down to a few basic principles. These principles could be extended to apply to any planetary juxtaposition obtaining at the moment of the question.

I began the study of horary astrology with an English translation of Neelakanta's **Prasna Tantra** by my father Dr. B.V. Raman, next took up the translations of Bhattotpala's **Prasagnana** and **Shatpanchasika** by late Sri S. Subramanya Sastri, then the rare Kerala classic **Prasna Marga** (Chapters 1 to 16) while it was in the process of being translated and revised by my father and finally came back to **Prasna Tantra**. Studying it over and over again, I pitched upon a fundamental principle that could answer any question. This principle, I found, lay in Ithasala Yoga, a combination of two planets in a particular way.

Other Yogas such as Easarapha, Kamboola, Nakta, Radda, etc., were but extensions and qualifications of this Yoga.

My father Dr. B.V. Raman has been my Guru in astrology. I have had the rare privilege of spending all my life so far with my Guru. These years have been field with astrological discussions on almost everything on earth ranging from the colour of one's dress to Marxism to Sankhya philosophy to marriage to success to death and even after life. These discussions have given me rare insights into the science of astrology which no book can offer. But what I have learnt can fill many books.

My mother Smt. Rajeswari Raman has also indirectly played the role of a Guru when she plied me with questions on just about everything under the sun. Trying to anser them was an exercise in horary planetary gymnastics which tested my interpretative ability.

I have sought to fill these pages with what I have learnt under my Guru and from my own experience of handling a wide range of cases.

A basic understanding of general astrology which includes casting the horoscope in necessary for a study of this book, if the principles outlined here are applied diligently, it should be quite easy to answer most questions. I trust all those genuinely interested in discovering truth will find this book useful.

I thank my brother Niranjan Babu of Sri Suprajaram for his constant help in reading proofs and for bringing out the book so neatly.

25-3-1979　　　　　　　　　　**Gayatri Devi Vasudev**

Contents

Foreword .... (v)

Preface to the Fourth Edition ....(vii)

Preface to the Fourth Edition .... (ix)

Preface to the First Edition .... (xi)

1. Branches of Astrology 1

2. Keys to the Signs 3

3. Keys to Houses 10

4. Keys to the Planets 19

5. Keys to Planets in Signs 27

6. Aspects 37

7. Reconciling Yogas and Tajaka Aspects 47

8. Question Data 51

9. How to Ask Questions 54

10. Significations, Malefics and Benefics 57

11. How to Read Aspects 61

12. The Role of the Moon and the Eleventh House 67

13. Some Exceptions 75

14. Timing Events 79

15. Bhava, Combustion, Nodes and Retrogression 85

16. Practical Illustrations 89

1
Branches of Astrology

Astrology is made up of 3 limbs. The are:

(1) Predictive astrology

(2) Mundane astrology

(3) Electional astrology

Predictive astrology is concerned with making forecasts or delineating future trends and possibilities. This branch can be further sub-divided into natal horoscopy and horary astrology. In the former, results are assessted on the basis of the chart erected for the time of birth. In horary astrology, the chart is erected for the time of question. Both give equally good results provided a careful balancing is made of all the factors in the chart. Our interest is horary astrology.

Mundane astrology is related to juding horoscopes of nations and of the collective destinies of peoples.

Electional astrology is predictive astrology reversed : Here a moment is so chosen as to ensure success of any venture begun at that moment. The chart is first cast and the event made to commence at the chosen time.

Horary astrology has been very popular, for it dispences away with the birth time which is sometimes not recorded at all or only vaguely noted down for a variety of reasons. However, if the birth chart can be made use of to study the entire life of the native, the horary chart is limited to assessing a particular situation with which the querent is concerned at the time of asking questions.

The greater part of horary astrology is very similar to natal astrology. The same signs of the Zodiac, the same significations of the twelve signs and houses are used in both. The only difference is the way in which aspects are judged and conclusions drawn.

2
Keys to the Signs

It is neceaary for a student to make himself thoroughly familiar with the signs, what they govern, the planets and their significations as well as the 12 Bhavas and what they indicate.

There are twelve signs of the Zodiac :

1. Aries ♈
2. Taurus ♉
3. Gemini ♊
4. Cancer ♋
5. Leo ♌
6. Virgo ♍
7. Libra ♎
8. Scorpio ♏
9. Sagittarius ♐
10. Capricon ♑
11. Aquarius ♒
12. Pisces ♓

♓	♈	♉	♊
♒			♋
♑			♌
♐	♏	♎	♍

Aries

Aries rules the head, forest, grazing grounds, hilly tracts, ceiling, stables, the East, brick-kilns, blacksmith. Aries natives have a broad and large forehead and a small chin. They are, the sign being fiery, thin, lean, tall and dry looking. Eyebrows are thick. The neck is thin and long like a goat's with medium hair on head. The skin is sallow and sometimes ruddy marked by spots and blemishes. They are hasty, impulsive and restless. They have an ability for leadership and are overbearing in nature. They are quick to lose their temper. Aries is fiery, moveable and dry.

Taurus

Taurus rules the face, fields, meadows, plains, cow-pens, low rooms, the ground floor, flowering shrubs and bushes, luxury halls, dining rooms, eating places. Taurus natives are handsome with a slightly snubby nose and broad cheeks. They are stout in body and height with thick necks, dark thick hair, fine teenth, large eyes and clear complexions. They are slow in movements and inclined to ease and luxury. They are suddenly and easily provoked to anger and do not cool down easily. They can be faithful and obedient, when they feel like it. Taurus is fixed and earthy.

Gemini

Gemini rules the neck and chest, bedrooms, walls, plastering, chests, trunks, boxes, barns, schools, study-rooms, colleges, electrical and electronic applicances, communication media such as cables, telephones, televisions, radio, the newspapers. Gemini natives are tall, well-built with flushy cheeks and face. They are, without exception, good-looking with clear and fair skins, thick lustrous hair, sensual lips. broad chest, good speakers, wilty, enquiring and curious, fond of knowledge, fun-seeking and given to quick changing moods and tempers. Gemini is common and airy.

Cancer

Cancer rules the heart, breast, watery fields, rivulets, small lakes, tanks, rivers, canals, local transports, wells, ditches, moats kitchen and homes, bakeries, milkbars, snackshops, pumps, places where food is stored. Cancer natives are small-built but fleshy, with attractive faces and eyes, soft curly but thick hair, plump limbs, emotional and possess deeply attached natures. Such natives are forgiving and try to act the mother in all their relationships. They are very sensitive but easily forget animosities. Cancer is moveable and watery.

Leo

Leo rules the belly, the digestive organs, the navel, mountains, thick forests, deep caves, woods, rocky terrain, deserts, palaces, parks, forts, fire-places, chimney, boilders and heat appliances, factories such as of iron and steel. Leo subjects have distinct jaws and joints that stand out with a head a little too large for the body. The body is thin, dry and hot in constitution. The limbs have no particular beauty about them but the carriage is royal and insolent. They have very great regard for themselves and get upset over mere trifles. They are domineering in nature and believe they are meant to pass only orders. The legs are thin but the trunk is large and wide. Leo is fiery and fixed.

Virgo

Virgo rules the hip, appendix, irrigated fields and channels, lush gardens, orchards plenty, corn fields, libraries, book shops, dairies, honey, farms and farmhouse, cottage produce. Virgo natives are the best looking of all the signs. They have dark fawn eyes, arching eyebrows, small attractive mouths, white even teeth and sharp determined chins. Limbs are graceful and tend towards corpulence. They mix easily with people. They are intelligent, sharp and good speakers. They get nervous easily and are weak in physical strength. They have studious and economizing habits. They avoid nasty situations through discretion and tact. Virgo is common and earthy.

Libra

Libra governs the groins, businessmen, market place, trade-centres, banks, hotels, amusement centre, public fetes and fairs, toilets, bathrooms, closets, water, tubs, flushouts, storeyed buildings. Those born in this sign are vivacious and sparkling in temperament and appearance. Either they are too balanced and wise or tend to lose balance over the nearest trifles. They are good talkers but sometimes rude, hasty and harsh. They are tall and elegant with slim bodies, pimpled or freckled skins, upright and judicious in their dealings. Libra is moveable and airy.

Scorpio

Scorpio rules the private parts, holes, deep caves, crevices, mines, underground celler, garages, carparks, the basement, sinks, swamps, ruins, garbage heaps, slush, moors, the lower shelves of a cupboard, panelled walls. Scorpio natives are small and neatly built with thick, bushy curly hair. They have dark bright eyes that have a hypnotic effect in them. They have dusky complexion and are usually bowlegged. They are offended easily and harbor ill-feelings. They can be the best of friends or the worst of enemies. They love to hide or run away from people and crowds. They are peevish but straightforward. Scorpio is fixed and watery.

Sagittarius

Sagittarius rules the thighs, royal and government quarters, government offices, armoury, racing grounds, gambling dens, the upper floors of buildings, stud-farms, race horses, vehicles, aircraft. Sagittarius natives are stout with broad shoulders, sparse hair, muscular limbs, straight nose, deep-set eyes, broad shanks and thighs. They are upright and honest in their dealings, easy going unless provoked, even tempered and genial hearted. They tend to take too many risks in life and are born gamblers. Sigittarius is common and fiery.

Capricorn

Capricorn rules the knees, watery places frequented by beasts, alligator, aquariums, fisheries, fishing nets, cowsheds, lumber houses, barren terrain, thorns, bushes, low-lying areas. Capricorn natives have an unusually long neck, small head, clear serious eyes, slender build. They are witty and changeable seeking perfection in everything with good organising capacities. They exhibit great patience and strength of will. They are cautious and secretive in nature. They are also ambitious, but at the same time, persevering and pragmatic. Capricorn is moveable and earthy.

Aquarius

Aquarius rules the ankles, pottery, ceramics, charity houses, stone quarries, laboratories, classrooms, sources of water and mountain springs. Aquarius subjects are tall, bony, with round faces and small eyes. They have small mouths and ill-formed or crooked teeth that often protrude. They have coarse hair and are sometimes slovenly. They are studious in habit and philosophical in temperament. They rarely lose their tempers, for, their attitude to life is stoic. They are honest and benevolent in disposition. Aquarius is fixed and airy.

Pisces

Pisces rules the feet, oceans, sea, hospitals, jails, maternity wards, nurses' quarters, breweries, bars and places of ill-repute, hermitages and concerts, water cisterns and tanks, coffee and tea-shops, ice-cream parlours. Pisces natives are short, plump and have beautiful faces. Their eyes are large, soft and lustrous, often brown or blue, hair wavy and light, eyebrows large, teeth good and complexion delicate. They are slow in their movements and lazy. They are too emotional and timid. They are irresolute, honest, fond of good food and company and often talkative. They are intuitive and psychic. Pisces is common and watery.

These significations of the signs are modified by the position of their lords and planets occupying and aspecting them. Fimilarity with these significations will enable one to make accurate predictions.

3
Keys to Houses

The Zodiac is 360° and is divied in 12 houses of 30 degrees each. The Ascendant is the first house and the other houses follow in succession. These twelve houses or Bhavas as they are called in Hindu astrology are given rulership over various sectors of life.

1 **The First House** or Bhava rules the querent, the body, its apperarance, health and strength, limbs, birth-place, antecedents, old age, happiness, misery, dignity, politics, tranquility, longevity, hair, pride, livelihood, skin, proficiency, avarice, insolence and arrogance, discontent, cattle, calumny from kinsmen, decorum, the state of an object the querent is interested in, sea-journeys, state of health, mind, the state of object of any question, and being the 12th from the 2nd, loss of family and food, being the 11th from the 3rd, gains of brothers and friends, being the 10th from the 4th, reputation of mother, family and home, social status of mother, being the 9th from the 5th journey and luck of children, being the 8th from the 6th, troubles of enemies and debtor, being the 7th from the 7th, affairs, health, appearance and interests of wife or husband, being the 6th from the 8th, illness of wife's or husband's family and relatives, being the 5th from the 9th, father's fortune, being the 4th from the 10th, career achievements and ambitions, being the 3rd from the 11th, journeys and co-borns of friends, and being the 2nd from the 12th, hospital bills, court fees and expenses on like account.

2 The Second House or Bhava rules eating, possessions, learning, food and drink, the right eye, face, moveable property, letter and documents speech, family, belief in tradition, nails, tongue, nose, money lent and being the 2nd from the 1st, all transactions involving money, being the 12th from the 3rd, lossess, hospitalization, imprisonment of brothers and neighbours, being the 11th from the 4th, social activities and profits of mother, being the 10th from the 5th, career interests of children, their reputation and performance in school or college, being the 9th from the 6th, journeys of maternal relatives, being 8th from the 7th, bequests and legacies through wife or husband being the 7th from the 8th, death of wife or husband, being the 6th from 9th, it shows the ill-health, debts and enenmies of father and preceptors the 5th from the 10th, shows investments and being speculation in career being the 4th from the 11th, it shows the homes of friends, and being the 3rd from the 12th, it shows short journeys of secret enemies.

3 The Third House or Bhava rules the right ear, courage and valour, brother, battle, legs, roadside places, mental confusion and conflicts, soldiers, wandering and short journeys, relatives, travel, correspondence, partition of property, female servants, neighbours and being the 12th from the 4th, shows losses, dreams and confinement or hospitalization of mother, occult practices, being the 2nd from the 3rd profits of brothers, being the 10th from the 6th, careers and occupation of enemies, their social standing and reputation, being the 9th from the 7th, shows partner's or husband's or wife's father, their long journeys and their religious and moral inclinations, being the 8th from the 8th, it shows life and rejuvenation, end of misfortune and afflictions, being the 7th from the 9th it shows father's trade associates, being the 6th from the 10th, litigation in relation to one's career or status, being the 5th from the 11th, it shows children of friends.

4 **The Fourth House** or Bhava rules house, land, maternal uncle, sister's son, vechicle, mother, cow, mines, lost articles, buffalo, kingdom, perfume, clothes, ornaments, the nadir, water, bridge, river, channels, education, school, small boats, goods name, milk, tents or pavilions, estates, gardens, digging ponds and wells, clarity of thought, clues to where stolen property is, abudance of corn, grain in wet lands and being the 12th from the 5th, loss in speculation and illness of children, being the 11th from the 6th, it shows the gains of enemies, friends of uncle, being the 10th from the 7th, the career of husband or wife, partner's social position, being the 9th from the 8th, it shows sudden luck as from lottery prizes and bequests, being the 8th from the 9th, father's inheritance, being the 7th from the 10th, husband or wife of career associates, being the 6th from the 11th, enemies and debts of friends, and being the 5th from the 12th, children of private enemies, their speculative gains and ventures.

5 **The Fifth House** rules tolls, taxes, minister, intelligence, children especially son, belly, customary laws, morals, love affairs, courtships, emotions, piety, father's good deeds, pregnancy, fertility and sterility, conception, speculation, garments, foresight, hereditary post, and being the 2nd from the 4th, income from mother, property, vehicles, lands, being the 3rd, brother's friends and neighbours, their journeys, being the 4th from the 2nd, family estates cars and domestic happiness, being the 6th from the 12th, problems of secret enemies, their sickness and imprisonment, being the 7th from the 11th, liaisons with associates and colleagues, being the 8th from the 10th, afflictions and losses in career, being the 9th from the 9th, grandfathers and grand uncles, being the 10th from the 8th, social background of wife or husband's family, being the 11th from the 7th, gains through trade and partnership, being the 12th from the 6th, secret foes and clandestine deals, losses of tenants and servants.

6 **The Sixth House** rules debts, arms, thieves, theft, wounds, disease, enemy, paternal relations, spells, magic incantations evil deeds, fear, humiliation, phlegm, swellings, insanity, anguish, untimely meals, falls, troubles from relatives, urinal trouble, dysentery, reproach, prison houses, service misunderstandings with brothers, tenants and servants and being the 2nd house from the 5th, it rules children's families, being the 3rd house from the 4th, uncles and aunts on the maternal side, being the 4th house from the 3rd, estates of neighbours, being the 5th house from the 2nd, luck through singing, speech and family trade, being the 7th from the 12th, affairs and sweethearts of private enemies, being the 8th house from the 11th, legacies of friends, being the 9th, house from the 10th, deputations and official journeys, transfers, being the 10th house from the 9th, father's career, being the 11th house from the 8th, death friends, being the 12th house from the 7th, the secret enmities and affairs of the wife or husband.

7 The Seventh House or Bhava rules wife or husband, desire, marriage, amorous affairs, engagements, unions, partner, appointment, road, path taken, course of action, people or public, chastity, flowers, sensual pleasures, virility, number of marriages, anus, trade, foreign residence, diplomacy, gift, destruction of power, overthrow of enemy, controversies, adopted son, and being the 2nd from the 6th, the wealth of enemies, profits through dealings with hospitals, jails and clinics, being the 3rd from the 5th, brothers of sweet-hearts, being the 4th from the 4th, property of mother, change of residence, being the 5th from the 3rd, nephews and nieces, being the 6th from the 2nd, family feuds, fugitives, being the 8th from the 12th, fines, pleas, death of enemies, being the 9th from the 11th, friend's antecedents and business gains, being the 10th from the 10th, distinction and merit in career, public service, and social and humanitarian projects, victories in battles and disputes, being the 11th from the 9th, father's personal effects, being the 12th from the 6th, detention and tracing of offenders, thieves and runaways.

8 The Eighth House or Bhava rules *Mangalya* or marital bond, mental pain, defeat, humiliation, longevity, scandals, impurities, obstacles, slaves, legacies, wills, death insurance bonuses, afflicted face, government punishment, loss of money, accidents, mutilation form, endless calamities, and being the 2nd from the 7th dowry, income through business and married partners, being the 3rd from the 6th, colleagues and sympathizers of one's enemies, being the 4th from the 5th, children's education and schools, being the 5th from the 4th, rules gains through literary talent, writing, being the 6th from the 3rd, brother's enemies and debts, being the 7th from the 2nd, substance of wife or husband, being the 9th from the 12th, antecedents of conspirators and foes, being the 10th from the 11th, careers and work of friends, being the 11th from the 10th, career gains, being the 12th from the 9th, father's hospitalization or political imprisonment and departure from ordained duties.

9 **The Ninth House** or Bhava rules preceptor foreign journeys, fortune, father, worship, legal matters, Dharmic acts, virtue, grandchild, nobility, generosity, *Teerthas* (centre of holy rivers), medicinal drugs, science, mental purity, acquisition of learning, affluence, policy, moral story, religious bathing, horses, elephants, prosperity, coronation, halls, town halls, assembly halls, circulation of money, and being the 2nd from the 8th, rules success of books, gains through insurance policies wife's or husband's relatives, being the 3rd from the 7th, letters of partnership, wife or husband's short journeys, being the 4th from the 6th properties of enemies, being the 5th from the 5th grandchildren and speculative gains of children, being the 6th from the 4th, mother's health, legal involvements and debts, being the 7th from the 3rd, brother's wife or sister's husband and disputes with brothers, being the 8th from the 2nd, pecuniary losses and complications, including hard-to-meet commitments, being the 10th from the 12th, the activities of foes, deceptive moves and conspiracies, being the 11th from the 11th, friends and their business profits, being the 12th from the 10th, losses and expenditure in career.

10 **The Tenth House** or Bhava rules commerce, rank or position, honour, occupation, success, fame, profession, sky, good conduct, quality, inclinations, gait, command, athletics, agriculture, doctor, thigh, honourable living, teaching, seal, of authority, subjection and being the 2nd from the 9th, father's income and family, being the 3rd from the 11th, brothers of and messengers from friends, being the 4th from the 7th, wife's or husband's mother, house and education, being the 5th from the 6th, children of tenants and servants, being the 6th from the 5th, private enemies of children and their ill-health, being the 7th from the 4th, mother's public activities, public trusts and educational institutions, being the 8th from the 3rd, death of brothers, their legacies, being the 9th from 2nd, general, fortune of the family, being the 11th from the 12th, friends and sympathisers of ill-wishes, and being the 12th from the 9th, father's expenditure and losses.

11 The Eleventh House or Bhava rules gains, income, acquisition, realization of objective, hopes, friends, acquaintances, profits, elder brothers and sister, daughter, pleasant tidings, dependency, gold, wealth, paternal property, pearls, ornaments, riches of every kind, ministership, awards, distinction, cooking, ear, shank, skill in art, important papers and documents of being the 2nd from the 10th, income from one's own excertions, being the 3rd from the 9th, paternal uncles and aunts, short journeys of and messages from father, being the 4th from the 8th, loss of mental tranquility, legal education, testators, secret and occult knowledge, being the 5th from the 7th, wife or husband's affairs and their business-investment profts, being the 6th from the 6th, enemies of enemies, sickness of servants, debts of tenants, being the 7th from the 5th, marriage or married spouse of son, being the 8th from the 4th, legacies from mother, being the 9th from the 3rd, foreign journeys of brothers, being the

10th from the 2nd, family reputation and standing, and being the 12th from the 12th, destruction of enemies, end of losses and regain of health.

12 **The Twelfth House** or Bhava governs sorrow, leg, left eye, loss, spy, tale-bearing, secrets, intrigues, end, poverty, sin, bed, imprisonment, awakening from sleep, discharge of debts, paternal wealth, enemy, entry into heaven, people's ire or mob fury, fetter, place of captivity, dispute, bodily injury, death, travelling or going away to another place, expenditure, loss of wife and being the 2nd from the 11th, invitations for dining with friends, being the 3rd from the 10th, journeys connected with career, being the 4th from the 9th, grandmother, ancestral property, sea-travels, being the 5th from the 8th, bequests and insurance investments relating to children, being the 6th from the 7th, wife's illness and conujugal life, being the 7th from the 6th, disputes with servants and tenants, being the 8th from the 5th, death and calamities to children such as kidnapping, being the 9th from the 4th, foreign education and residence, being the 10th from the 3rd, brother's career and being the 11th from the 2nd, family circle of relatives and family friends.

If the 3rd house denotes the first brother, the 3rd therefrom denotes the brother after him or his younger brother, the 3rd therefrom, the 3rd younger brother and so on. Similarly, if the 5th house denotes the first child, the third therefrom denotes the 2nd child, the 3rd from here, the third child and so on. If the 11th house denotes the eldest brother, the 3rd therefrom namely, the 2nd denotes his younger brother. This way, you can, with a little practice, manage to find any relationship, no matter how distant, in the chart

Significations relating to various Bhavas can be easily made out.

Suppose, the querent is worried about his friend's missing son. The Ascendant denotes the querent, the 11th house denotes the friend and the 5th therefrom, the missing boy.

	Aries		
Lagna Aquarius	Chart 1 Rasi		
Sagittarius			

In this illustration (Chart 1) the Ascendant Aquarius rules the querent. The 11th house, namely Sagittarius, shows the friend whose child is missing. The 5th house from the 11th house, that is, Aries, denotes the missing boy. Or, in other words, as you have already seen, the 3rd house governs friend's children.

4
Keys to the Planets

Now, we move on to the keys to the planets. We all know although commonly referred to as planets, we are really speaking of Grahas of which nine are important to our study. They are :

1. Sun
2. Moon
3. Mars
4. Mercury
5. Jupiter
6. Venus
7. Saturn
8. Rahu
9. Ketu

These planets have innumerable properties with which you must get acquainted. But these properties are neither astronomical nor physical. They are esoteric in significane.

Sun

The sun governs copper, gold, brass, valuables, father, heart (the organ), vitality, anything auspicious, the soul, fame, glory, courage, victory, government and quasi-government service, Greeshma or summer, Lord Siva, forests, mountaineering, participation, in Homas and Yagnas, temples, physician, king, officiating priest at a sacrifice, minister, tiger, deer and goose, royal patronage, half-a-year, eyes, roaming, timber, head ailments, stones, public activity, river banks, ruby, capturing the enemy, thick cord, saffron, hostility, anger that does not cool down easily palatial buildings and apartments.

The Sun is described as being bilious in temperament, thinning hair, sparse eyelashes and eyebrows, dark red in hue, eyes tinted red, clad in red garments and well-built with strong bones. He is wrathful with huge arms.

Siva temples, open fields, courtyards allowing plentry of light, dry regions without any water and the Eastern quarter are the haunts of the Sun.

Moon

The Moon rules mother, her welfare, mind, sea-bath, Varsha or monsoon, umbrella, fans, fruits, tendencies, flowers, corn, farming, pearls, bell-mental, silver, sweet flavor, milk, cloth, water, fountains, sewers, seaports, cow women, good food, bodily health, beauty, rounded contours, worshippers of Sasta (Harihara), females, washermen, farmers, aquatic, animals, hare, antelope, crane, partridge.

The moon has a large body and is sometimes old. He is lean, fair, has lovely soft light eyes (brown or blue), and fine soft but thin hair. He rules theblood. He speaks softly, wears white and has a clear, delicate, dewy complexion. He has wind and phlegm and is mild in temperament.

The Moon also rules intelligence, perfume, fortress, Brahmin, idleness and ease, epilepsy, spleen, sourness, sugarcane, typhoid, swelling, consumption, waistband, salt, short stature, autumn, an interval of 48 minutes, facial radiance, wheat, curds, people, foreign travel royal insignia, serpent, silken garments, crystals and delicate textures of cloth, commodities, kitcher-ware, cutlery and crockery.

The Moon's haunts are places of worship of Goddess Parvati, women's quarters, places where water is found – kitchens, toilets, customs, tanks, and herbs planets and places where liquor is kept as in distilleries. He rules the North-west.

Mars

Mars rules strength, valour, brother, products, derived from the earth, cruelty and hatred, odium, fire, kitchen, gold, relatives, weapons, thieves, physical vigour and stamina, falsehood, furnaces, bakeries, butchery, commander-in-chief, wounds bleeding, bollts, cooks and chefs, arms-bearer, goldsmith, ram, cook, jackal, monkey, vulture.

Mars also shows loss of virility, red wines, enemy, trumpet, quadruped, fool, anger, foreign travel, heat, service under a king (government), automobiles, machinery, tin, arms like swords, spears, lances, knives, guns, youth, pungent, assembly-hall, calumny and gossip, flesh eating, Greeshma or summer, Brahma, forester, village headman, rogue, leanness, skill in archery, **Sama Veda**, icon, management of wild animals, independence, assertive nature, haemorrhage, persistence, restlessness, drying of blood, mounting vehicles, coral, laboratories.

Mars is described as being well-built with a slim waist and curly lustrous hair. He has fierce eyes but a youthful look. He is bilious in temperament and cruel. He dresses in red clothes and is ruddy is complexion. He is generous and rules marrow.

Mars frequents the underworld, hide-outs of thieves or of vulgar people, mines, battle-fields, places with fire and the South. He comes under Lord Subramanya.

Mercury

Mercury governs learning, speech, eloquence, skill in fine arts, maternal uncle, religiousness, all intellectual pursuits, sacrifice, rites relating to Maha Vishnu, truth, oyster-shells, places of recreation, skill in electric and electronic subject, scientific instruments, stationery, pens and writing articles relations, friends, humour, wit sister's child, cowherd, pundit, artisan, accountant, Vishnu devotees, Garuda, parrot, cat, horses, treasury, mathematics, writing, Brahmin, Sudra, infantry, huge bungalows, green, sculpture, astrology temples, Vedanta philosophy, maternal grandfather and paternal relations, eunuch, emerald, child, renunciation, Hemanta (winter), navel, proficiency in languages, **Atharvana Veda**, reproductive organ, impartiality, skill in testing and judging precious stones, prayers, incantations, spells, tenniscourts, attorney's office, clerical jobs, bills.

Mercury governs the skin and is grass green in colour. He is evenly built and has all the 3 humours of phlegm, wind and bile. His veins are prominent and he has red long eyes. His garment is green. He talks amicably.

Mercury is found in places of learning like schools, colleges, libraries, Sri Vishnu temples, places of recreation and in the North.

Jupiter

Jupiter presides over knowledge, virtues, progeny, counsellors and ministers, conduct, dissemination of knowledge, magnanimity, learning in the **Vedas**, Sastras, **Smritis** and sacred lore, prosperity and abudance in everything, penance, respect for elders and devotion to God and the wise, treasury the sense organs and their conquest, husband's welfare, renunciate important persons, religious and monastic heads, pigeon, swan horse, one's ordained duty, cars, cows, savings, Meemamsa philosophy, astrology, dropsy, grandfather and grandchild, eldest brother, mansion, winter, thigh, royal or national honours, friends, oratorial talent, fat, holy water, towering building, *lapis lazauli*, caparisoned vehicles, honey, oil, silk.

Corpulent with a broad chest, Jupiter has a paunch. He is yellow in colour with brown eyes and hair. He has a powerful voice that is clear. He is intelligent, phlegmatic and interested in money.

He is found in treasuries, banks, near *Aswattha* or peepal tree, temples, churches, monasteries, dwelling places of the pious and in the North-east, Hemanta or winter, courts of justice and wardrobes.

Venus

Venus rules wealth, vehicles, clothes, mansion, ornaments, hoarded goods, music, dance, instruments of music, wife, happiness, scents, flowers, sexual indulgence, couch, poetry, sport and amusement, sensuousness, counsellor, charming speech, marriage festivities, merchant, weaver, dancer, musician, prostitutes, call-girls, peacock, buffalo, parrot, cow, whiteness, silver, diamond, ogling, Vaisya, beauty, middle age, Veena, lute, flute and other musical instruments, running after women, semen, truth, stage and screen, skill in love-making, classical dance, Goddess Parvati or Lakshmi, emaciation, mother during day-time, genital organ, ornaments.

Venus is well-built and tall with beautifully proportioned limbs. He has thick, black curly hair and large broad attractive eyes. He wears a multi-coloured garment. He is virile and of the colour of the *Durva*. His temperament is a mixture of phlegm and wind.

Venus is found in the harem, theatres, cinema, hotels, women's quarters, prostitute houses, dancing halls, bedrooms and in the South-east. Venus rules Vasanta or spring.

Saturn

Saturn rules life, longevity, destiny, evolution, fear, degradation, sickness, penury, labour and labourer, manual work, sin, impurity, constancy and loyalty, servitude, debts, fetters, iron, brooms, dusters, agricultural implements, out-houses, captivity, prisons, oil-monger, black colour, hunter, blacksmith, elephant, crow, cuckoo, out-caste, maid-servant, ass, donkey, handsome looks, the lowest caste, woods, birds, a life lacking in virtue, tendons, Sisira Ritu or winter, an illegitimate child, one born to a lowly woman, a year, Sudra, Vaisya, father, blanket, cousin, downfall, oil, ignorance, rulership, goats, buffalo, fondness for sexual pleasure, worshipper of God Yama, the supernatural, sodium, iron, sapphire.

Saturn is tall, lean, stooping with prominent bones and teeth, coarse hair and thick, bushy eye-brows, lame, dark. The veins and arteries stand out, he is idle, slothy, fond of back-biting. He is full of wind. He governs the muscle. He is cold-hearted with no compassion, dirty, fierce and angry. He is old and wears black.

His haunts are the dwelling places of the lowly and the vulgar, the labour class and slothful. He rules the West, and lives in Muniswara's temples, desert, obscure and remote places, dilapidated structures, garbage heaps and dustbins.

Rahu

Rahu rules umbrella, kingdom, fallacious argument, bitter stinging speech, outcaste, wicked woman, degenerate, an heretic, heterodoxy, South, festering sores, boils and eruptions, mountains, confusion, exile, wind, phlegm, sorrow, snakes and serpents, reptiles, dream interpretation, occult and psychic abilities, Goddess Durga, masochism, co-habitation with animals, homo-sexuality, lesbianism, air.

Rahu is found in ant-hills, tunnels, graveyards, tombs, caves and Buddhists, snake-charmer, ass, ram, wolf, darkness, mosquito, bug, insect, owl are all under Rahu's rulership.

Rahu, besides, carries all the characteristics of Saturn.

Ketu

Ketu governs doctor, dog, cock, salvation, wealth, treasure, pain, grief, hyper-sensitivity, dips in sacred rivers, witchcraft and black magic, science, knowledge of the soul, silence, luxury, luck, trouble from enemies, poor eating habits, indifference, hunger, stomach-pain, skin eruptions, spiritual *Sadhana*, worship of Siva and Ganesha, Sudra, courting arrest.

Ketu is also found in ant-hills, holes, tunnels, and in darkness. Buddhists, snake-charmer, ass, wolf, serpents also come under Ketu.

Ketu is, in addition, similar to Mars.

5
Keys to Planets in Signs

Different planets in different signs give different results. The characteristics of the sign and planet blend to give a mixed result which generally describes the querent or the person the querent is interested in depending upon the house or Bhava in which a sign falls.

Planets in Aries

The Sun in Aries gives medium height, bright complexion, thinning hair, blood-shot eyes, stained teeth and noble carriage.

The Moon in Aries gives slightly plump, medium build, fine thin hair, freckled complexion and restless eyes.

Mars in Aries gives a well-built, large boned look with thick eye-brows, thick hair, fierce look, ruddy complexion and an air of confidence.

Mercury in Aries gives medium height, an indifferent complexion, oval face, sharp witty eyes which could be tricky.

Jupiter in Aries gives medium height, thick hair, sharp nose, tending towards corpulence, not very smart-looking but of pleasant disposition.

Venus in Aries gives thick curly hair, large dark darting eyes, slender build and generally attractive, but assertive nature.

Saturn in Aries gives moderate height, coarse hair, sparse body hair, prominent features and an ill-disposed, peevish nature.

Planets in Taurus

The Sun in Taurus gives a short but stocky stature with dark complexion, broad cheeks and not too thick hair, stubborn and self-willed nature.

The Moon in Taurus gives medium height, fleshy cheeks with straight nose and neat features, clear complexion with a stubborn nature.

Mars in Taurus gives medium height, thick coarse hair, dark complexion and an assertive, self-willed nature.

Mercury in Taurus gives medium height, corpulent build, slothful habits and callousness in everything.

Jupiter in Taurus gives medium height, stout, strong body, fair complexion, light eyes, curly hair and an ease-loving nature.

Venus in Taurus gives handsome features with lustrous eyes, medium height, fleshy face and a friendly honest disposition.

Saturn in Taurus gives clumsy carriage, slouching posture, dark hair, grave expression and rough manners.

Planets in Gemini

The Sun in Gemini gives a well-built body, sanguine complexion, balding hair, sparse eye-lashes and well-mannered disposition.

The Moon in Gemini gives good height, corpulence, round big eyes, clear fair complexion and an inquiring nature.

Mars in Gemini gives good height with proportionate limbs, swarthy complexion and a wandering, restive nature.

Mercury in Gemini gives a good body with height and carriage, ingenious looks and conversational ability.

Jupiter in Gemini gives a full, plump build of medium height or slightly more, blemishes in complexion, brownish hair and a gentle mannered disposition.

Venus in Gemini gives good height, good eyes, fairly good complexion, thick, luxuriant hair and slender build with sociable habits and manner.

Saturn in Gemini gives tall stature, thick hair, piercing deep-set eyes and an argumentative nature.

Planets in Cancer

The Sun in Cancer gives small stature, corpulence, dull and thinning hair, small sharp eyes and a cheery nature.

The Moon in Cancer gives a plump, short, homely face, round stature with thick hair, round eyes, kind and gentle disposition.

Mars in Cancer gives a dull complexion, short stature, thick hair, contentious and restless disposition.

Mercury in Cancer gives short stature, dull hair and dark complexion, roving sharp eyes and a self-opinionated disposition.

Jupiter in Cancer gives fleshy middle stature with fair and rosy cheeks, brownish hair and fussy nature.

Venus in Cancer gives a fleshy body of medium height, dark thick hair, indolent, sensual but attractive eyes and a vain disposition.

Saturn in Cancer gives short ill-formed stature with very dark complexion and grizzly hair. The eyes are neurotic and malicious looking.

Planets in Leo

The Sun in Leo gives medium or short height, strong, wiry body with light brown hair, sanguine complexion, proud in bearing and carriage.

The Moon in Leo gives tall stature, brown eyes, angular jaws and features with a lofty and aspiring nature.

Mars in Leo gives a well-built body with Sun-burnt complexion, large eyes and confident and quick gait with a passionate and free-spirited disposition.

Mercury in Leo gives round face and a high nose, medium build, brown eyes and a boastful disposition.

Jupiter in Leo gives tall and well-built physique tending to corpulence, curly hair, ruddy complexion and a disposition that is haughty and magnanimous.

Venus in Leo gives clear complexion, round face with fine eyes, fairly thick hair, firm and neat built with tall stature and an angry but generous disposition.

Saturn in Leo gives tall stature with big-boned limbs and thinning hair, thick bushy eye-brows and grave disposition.

Planets in Virgo

The Sun in Virgo gives a tall, slender frame with thick dark hair and a pleasant and agreeable nature.

The Moon in Virgo gives medium stature, rather dark complexion, serious but ingenious mentality with a tendency to boast.

Mars in Virgo gives a well-built medium stature with dark thick hair, a ruddy complexion with a scar or mark on the face, an energetic and able nature.

Mercury in Virgo gives a tall frame with alert and sparkling eyes that are witty. Hair is thick and build is tall and well-proportioned.

Jupiter in Virgo gives a heavy, corpulent frame with an ordinary complexion, a boastful but studious and ambitious nature.

Venus in Virgo gives a dark complexion with an oval face, bright keen eyes and a clever but cunning disposition that is not always lucky.

Saturn in Virgo gives spare tall stature, dark hair, sad eyes and a long face with a gloomy melancholic disposition.

Planets in Libra

The Sun in Libra gives a tall, slender frame, fair but blemished complexion light hair, a refined and polite disposition.

The Moon in Libra gives attractive features in a full face, bright fine complexion and a jovial fun-loving disposition.

Mars in Libra gives a well-built body with a ruddy complexion, rather light hair, with a cheerful but conceited nature.

Mercury in Libra gives medium height with well-proportioned limbs, light eyes, quite thick hair and an eloquent and courteous nature.

Jupiter in Libra gives a tall frame, fair complexion with fleshy plump cheeks and limbs and pimpled complexion. The nature is mild but winning.

Venus in Libra gives an oval face, with deep brown or black eyes, thick, glossy hair, freckled face, and a tall graceful figure with a sunny fair disposition.

Saturn in Libra gives a build of medium height with thick, dark hair, high forehead, and a quiet and unassuming nature.

Planets in Scorpio

The Sun in Scorpio gives small dark eyes with thick-set eye-brows that tend to grow sparse with age, a swarthy complexion and a strong determined disposition.

The Moon in Scorpio gives a plump short stature with thick hair, dull complexion and an ill-disposed, malicious nature.

Mars in Scorpio gives a rugged, well-built muscular body, broad cheeks, ruddy complexion and thick, curly hair with a passionate, revengeful but inventive mind.

Mercury in Scorpio gives medium height, broad shoulders, indifferent but curly hair and complexion, and a crafty, deceitful, quarrelsome nature.

Jupiter in Scorpio gives a stout, short, fleshy frame with dull eyes and complexion and a selfish pompous nature.

Venus in Scorpio gives a stout, voluptuous body with dusky hair and complexion, vicious and sensual looking eyes and a jealous and catty disposition.

Saturn in Scorpio gives short stature with dark complexion, very curly grizzly hair, broad shoulders and a disposition that retains anger.

Planets in Sagittarius

The Sun in Sagittarius gives a tall, handsome body with sparse brown hair, fair complexion and an ambitious but philosophical outlook.

The Moon in Sagittarius gives attractive features and a well-proportioned body with a bright gleaming complexion and a hasty, ambitious but kind nature.

Mars in Sagittarius gives a tall, well-built frame with deep penetrating eyes, brown hair and an independent and hasty disposition.

Mercury in Sagittarius gives a tall well-formed and proportionate body with fair, smooth complexion, light eyes and a beaked nose. The disposition is hasty, imprudent but easily appeased.

Jupiter in Sagittarius gives a healthy, ruddy complexion with a heavy but tall frame, large eyes and features, a magnanimous and friendly nature.

Venus in Sagittarius gives a tall, good looking body with thick hair and bright, dark eyes and a passionate but obliging disposition.

Saturn in Sagittarius gives a large bony frame with good complexion, grave but kindly eyes and a helpful sympathetic nature.

Planets in Capricorn

The Sun in Capricorn gives medium height and an indifferent appearance with thin body, sparse hair, dull complexion but an honourable and agreeable disposition.

The Moon in Capricorn gives a small weak frame with thin, sad face, dull eyes, thin neck and dark hair. The disposition is crafty, unreliable and debauched.

Mars in Capricorn gives thick dark hair, short frame and small features with an ambitious and dynamic personality.

Mercury in Capricorn gives a small, mean body with sharp, suspicious eyes and a narrow, crafty and tricky nature.

Jupiter in Capricorn gives small stature, pale and sallow complexion and eyes, sparse facial and bodily hair with a peevish, inactive, discontented nature.

Venus in Capricorn gives medium height with a pale complexion and dark eyes. The disposition is indolent but ambitious and fond of enjoyment.

Saturn in Capricorn gives a lean, bony body with dark coarse straight hair, small penetrating eyes and an avaricious, discontented nature.

Planets in Aquarius

The Sun in Aquarius gives medium height and build tending to corpulence with round eyes, clear complexion and light hair, with an ambitious nature that seeks to rule in all activities of life.

The Moon in Aquarius gives a well-formed body of medium height with clear brown and large eyes, thin hair and rather more bodily hair. The disposition is friendly, thoughtful and ingenious.

Mars in Aquarius gives a tall well-built body with a reddish complexion and sandy hair with a restless, assertive but refined nature.

Mercury in Aquarius gives medium build and height, fleshy face and clear friendly eyes with a humane, pleasing kind nature.

Jupiter in Aquarius gives a corpulent body of medium height, clear complexion and not too thick or dark hair with a disposition that is helpful, bright and happy-go-lucky.

Venus in Aquarius gives a beautiful body, clear complexion with soft, brownish hair, a courteous disposition and concern for others.

Saturn in Aquarius gives medium height, dark hair and deep-set piercing eyes and sober, dignified carriage with a well-disposed, refined nature and an ingenious mind.

Planets in Pisces

The Sun in Pisces gives medium height, stout build and a clear complexion with rounded features. The disposition is generous but the nature tends to prodigality.

The Moon in Pisces gives a plump, clumsy body with soft eyes, fleshy cheeks and lips and a dull, lazy but sympathetic disposition.

Mars in Pisces gives a plump body of medium stature, dull complexion, restless eyes and a wavering, idling mind with an inclination to vicious habits.

Mercury in Pisces gives an awkward body and gait with shuffling feet, nervous eyes, thin dull hair and a conceited, talkative nature that is addicted to women and drinking.

Jupiter in Pisces gives medium height with moderately good looks, full face and dark hair a studious, ambitious disposition and fondness for pleasure.

Venus in Pisces gives middle stature, plump face with attractive cheeks and eyes, full lips, clear and radiant complexion with a peaceful, mild and just disposition.

Saturn in Pisces gives medium height, large raw-boned limbs, small eyes, indifferent teeth with an unreliable, treacherous disposition.

These characteristics of planets can be used in describing the querent and the person quesited about. The rising sign, the planets in it and aspecting it and the sign occupied by the Ascendant lord describe the querent. Similarly, the sign signifying the quesited together with its lord and the planets influencing these two factors give a reasonably fair description of the person.

6
Aspects

A horary chart is interpreted on the basis of aspects. These aspects are different from aspects we come across in Parasari astrology. The aspects employed in horary astrology are called Tajaka aspects and are similar to aspects in Western astrology.

The nature, good or bad, of aspects is determined not by the planets but by the degree of aspects.

The following aspects are important to us :

Conjunction	0°
Semi-sextile	30°
Sextile	60°
Square	90°
Trine	120°
Opposition	180°

The conjunction is caused when 2 planets are in the same degree and it may be benefic or malefic.

The semi-sextile is caused between two planets 30° apart and is feebly benefic, there being promise of desired results if prompt and persevering effort is put forth.

The sextile is caused (Triteeya Ekadasi or 3-11 positions) by 2 planets being 60° apart and is benefic and with a little effort, the desired objective may be gained.

The trine is caused by 2 planets being 120° apart (in mutual trines or Trikonas) and is an excellent aspect indicating favorable outcome of the subject of the query.

Next, we come to the malefic or hostile aspects.

The square is caused by 2 planets being 90° apart (in Kendras or 4-10), and denotes stress, opposition and hurdles but not necessarily failure.

The opposition is also malefic caused by 2 planets being 180° apart (Samasaptama or 7-7) and indicates sheer hopelessness and impossibility of achieving the desired result.

	Mars 18°		Jupiter 18°
Mercury 18% Sun 18°	Chart 2 Rasi		
Venus 18°			Saturn 18°
	Moon 18°		

In Chart 2, the Sun and Mercury are in conjunction.

The Sun and Venus are in semi-sextile. The Sun and Mars are sextile. The Sun and Jupiter are in trine. The Sun and Moon are in square. The Sun and Saturn are in opposition.

But we do not always, in fact, only very rarely, come across exact degree aspects as in the example. The planets are invariably a little behind or a little ahead of exact aspects.

So, we have orbs of influence beyond which the influence of a planet ceases to be effective in considering aspects.

According to Neelakanta's **Prasna Tantra**, the following are the orbs of influence:

Sun	15°
Moon	12°
Mars	8°
Mercury	7°
Jupiter	9°
Venus	7°
Saturn	9°

If the aspect is exact, it is called perfect or partile and poses no problems. Otherwise, this is what we do. The orbs of influence of the two planets are added and divided by 2 to get the average orb of influence. If the aspect is beyond this orb, there is no real aspect. If it falls within the average orb, the aspect is effective, though not exact or partile and is called platic.

Although we could use this average method for such strong aspects as the trine, opposition or conjunction, it would be better to employ a smaller orb for the lesser aspects. A general orb of 6° 40' or 2 Padas can be allowed for all aspects, the weaker as well as the stronger ones, to be able to come to conclusions safely.

	\multicolumn{2}{c}{**Chart 3** **Rasi**}	
		Mars 3° Venus 12°	

Both Venus and Mars, in Chart 3, are in the same sign but the distance between them is too much to consider them in conjunction. The planets are separated by more than 7° which is the average of their orbs of influence $(7 + 8)/2 = 7½$. They are, therefore, not in conjunction.

Although, it is the arc of aspect that decides its benefic or malefic nature, we must also take into account the planets involved. A square between Jupiter and the Moon would not give an unfavorable result or failure of the same intensity as in the case of Mars and Saturn. In the latter, the blow could be sudden, explosive and shattering and in the former, the failure may come in a quite sort of manner.

The Tajaka system gives some definitions of aspects which are very effective in making predictions. These are the aspects proper in horary astrology.

They are:

(1) Ithasala

(2) Easarapha

(3) Nakta

(4) Yamaya

(5) Kamboola

Ithasala

An Ithasala Yoga is caused when a faster planet with less longitude is behind a slower planet with more longitude. This is a benefic Yoga.

In Chart 4, the Moon is in Ithasala with Saturn indicating a favorable outcome in relation to the significations of the houses (Bhavas) involved.

		Moon 16°	
	Chart 4 Rasi		Saturn 18°
Lagna			

When the Ithasala occurs within half a degree, it becomes Muthaseela, a very favorable aspect.

Easarapha

When a faster planet with greater longitude is ahead of a slower planet with less longitude, an Easarapha Yoga is formed. This is an unfavorable aspect.

In Chart 5, Mercury, the faster planet, is ahead of the slower Jupiter forming an Easarapha. This indicates failure or the object of the query becoming a thing of the past.

These two aspects correspond to the applying and separating aspects of Western astrology. In Ithasala Yoga, the faster planet applies to the slower planet while in Easarapha, the faster planet separates from the slower planet. The Moon being the fastest of all planets can apply to all other planets.

		Jupiter 6° Mercury 19°	
	Chart 5 **Rasi**		
Lagna			

The Moon can apply to Mercury, Venus, the Sun, Mars, Jupiter and Saturn.

Mercury can apply to Venus, the Sun, Mars, Jupiter and Saturn.

Venus can apply to the Sun, Mars, Jupiter and Saturn.

The Sun can apply to Mars, Jupiter and Saturn.

Mars can apply to Jupiter and Saturn.

Jupiter can apply only to Saturn.

Nakta Yoga

When there is no aspect between 2 planets but a planet faster than the two is in aspect to both, it causes an aspect between the two or transfers light from the faster planet to the slower planet.

		Lagna	
Jupiter 9°	Chart 6 Rasi		
	Venus 14°		Moon 7°

In Chart 6, there is no aspect between Jupiter and Venus but the Moon is in Ithasala with both. So, he establishes a link between Venus and Jupiter with the same result as if the two had been in Ithasala. The result will be fulfilment of the object signified by Venus and Jupiter and the houses or Bhavas involving them through the agency of the Bhava signified by the Moon.

Lagna	Mercury 8°		
	Chart 7 Rasi		Mars 16°
		Jupiter 10°	

In Chart 7, Mercury is applying to an opposition of Jupiter and a square of Mars. There is no aspect between Jupiter and Mars but Mercury translates light from Mars to Jupiter in the process generating a square aspect between Mars and Jupiter and signifying failure through the Bhava Mercury signifies.

Yamaya Yoga

When there is no aspect between two planets and a slower planet is in aspect with each of them, it (the slower planet) transfers light from the faster of the two planets to the other.

	Mercury 20°		
	Chart 8 Rasi		
Lagna			
Jupiter 21°			Venus 14°

In Chart 8, Mercury is in Ithasala with Jupiter. Venus is in Ithasala with Jupiter. But Mercury and Venus, to whose houses the question relates, are not in Ithasala. Jupiter transfers light from Mercury to Venus so that they act as if in Ithasala and promote the object of the query.

In Chart 9, Venus and Mars are not in any aspect but both are separately in square and opposition respectively to jupiter. The result is the same as would be if Mars and Venus were in square aspect indicating unfavorable results pertaining to houses signified by Venus and Mars.

Chart 9 Rasi

		Mars 2°	
	Chart 9 Rasi		
			Venus 15°
Lagna	Jupiter 18°		

Kamboola Yoga

When there is Ithasala between two planets and the Moon is also in Ithasala with both of them, Kamboola Yoga is formed. This is a favorable Yoga.

In Chart 10, the Moon is in Ithasala with Mars and Venus both of whom are in Ithasala with each other generating a Kamboola Yoga.

Mars 18°			
	Chart 10 Rasi		Lagna Moon 11°
	Venus 16°		

The last three Yogas of Nakta, Yamaya and Kamboola correspond to collection of light in Western astrology according to which when a planet receives the aspects of any two other planets, without themselves being in aspect, the first forwards light (or aspect) from the one to the other of the non-aspecting planets.

We have seen how to assess Yogas or aspects between planets in direct motion. We now go to retrograde planets.

Radda Yoga

A Yoga between retrograde planets (one or both or all involved) is called Radda Yoga.

When a retrograde planet is involved in an Ithasala Yoga, the result would be favorable after much difficulty.

Radda Yoga also includes combust planets in Ithasala when the result is success after initial and seeming difficulty or impossibility.

Lagna		Jupiter (R) 8°	
		Chart 11 **Rasi**	
Saturn 12° Sun 7°			

In Chart 11, Saturn in combustion and retrograde Jupiter are both in Ithasala with each other and the Sun as well forming a Radda Yoga.

7
Reconciling Yogas and Tajaka Aspects

We have just learnt the semi-sextile, the sextile and trine are benefic aspects while the opposition is malefic. Conjunction can be benefic or malefic. The square can be benefic but with too many difficulties on the way.

But we have also seen that Ithasala Yogas are indicative of gaining the objective of the query while Easarapha indicates disappointment.

How do we combine these aspects and Yogas for delineating results?

The benefic aspects indicate harmonious working of events and relatively easy and smooth progress. The malefic or hostile aspects mean obstacles and stress in the smooth flow of events. But success or otherwise of an object does not depend upon either of these aspects which only show the nature of progress in achieving the objective. They do not indicate failure or success. It is only the Yogas, Ithasala and Easarapha, that indicate success and failure respectively.

In Chart 12, the question relates to marriage. The houses involved are the Lagna and the 7th house. The planets ruling them, Venus and Mars, are in square aspect but in Ithasala. This would imply the marriage in question would take place but in the face of much opposition and tension. The square aspect also indicates married life would be marked by tension and would be no bed of roses.

Mars 12°	**Chart 12** **Rasi**	
	Venus 6°	Lagna

In Chart 13, relating to whether a job can be secured, Mercury and Jupiter denote the Bhavas involved, namely, the Ascendant and the 10th house. The planets are in trine in Ithasala indicating an unexpected opportunity for a job turning up and the querent being fully satisfied and happy with the job on securing it.

	Mercury 20°		
	Chart 13 **Rasi**		Jupiter 25°
Lagna			

In Chart 14, where the question relates to a contemplated foreign journey, Jupiter indicating

Reconciling Yogas and Tajaka Aspects

querent and 9th lord Mars ruling foreign journey are in conjunction but in Easarapha Yoga. The result would be the journey not coming off as planned.

Lagna		Mars 12° Jupiter 3°	
	Chart 14 **Rasi**		

In Chart 15, the question relates to acquisition of a certain sum of money ruled by the 2nd lord Sun. The Sun and Ascendant lord Moon are in trine but there is no Ithasala between the two indicating the querent would not get the amount.

Moon 21°			
	Chart 15 **Rasi**		Lagna
	Sun 12°		

The opposition, whether Ithasala or Easarapha, is generally unfavorable and an exception to the rule we have just learnt.

In Chart 16, the question is whether a particular marriage will come through. Mercury ruling the Ascendant and Jupiter, the 7th house, are the planets involved. Mercury is applying to an opposition to Jupiter. The marriage would not, therefore, take place and the parties will withdraw or break the engagement gracefully, since both planets are benefic.

			Lagna
	Chart 16 Rasi		Mercury 17°
Jupiter 20°			

For the same question in Chart 17, the planets involved being the Sun and Saturn, the answer would be negative. The parties would separate with much bitterness and anger, the planets being malefic Saturn and the Sun.

		Sun 16°	
Lagna	Chart 17 Rasi		
	Saturn 14°		

8
Question Data

*A*strology — *30 Years Research* has something interesting to tell us of Horary Astrology:

> Research has convinced us that in judging a mental event (formulating a definite, precise question about one single matter in which the person asking is deeply interested and strongly desirous of an answer), the same natal astrological rules apply. While the question is being formulated, the mental event is under gestation, even as a child undergoes a period of gestation. When the question is asked, it manifests externally moving from the mental to the physical world even as a child at birth moves into the external world from the womb of the mother. Thus, from an astrological point of view, the birth of a question or idea is the moment when it is expressed verbally or in writing.
>
> A chart erected for the time such a mental event is born will reveal as much about it...as the chart of a child will reveal about its character and the events it may attract.
>
> In a horary question, it is essential that the individual have an intense desire to know the answer about some one thing. More than one question, asked at the same time, brings a multiple birth of mental

events, resulting in imperfect births. If there is not an intense desire to know the answer, the mental event does not have sufficient vitality to live, and, therefore, the expected results are not apt to be realized.

Now we come to the data of the question. Which is the time of question? It is the date, time and place at which the question expresses itself.

1. If you approach an astrologer personally, the moment when you voice your question before him becomes the question time.

2. If you write to him from a local place, you can write down the time at which you begin the letter which becomes the question time.

3. If the letter is from an outside city or town or place, the question time remains the same but the place of question is the place where the letter is written and not where it is received.

4. When you write the letter from outside the city or place of the astrologer and have failed to jot down the time or date of question, the time, date and place where the astrologer reads (not receives) the letter becomes the question time.

5. When you put a local call to an astrologer, the place, time and date are common to both and become the question data.

6. When you put a call from a different city, the time and date are common but the place of question becomes the place where you receive the call.

7. When you call up an astrologer from a different country, the time, date and place are those at the place of receiving the call.

8. Suppose, a man puts an international call from New York, United States, to an astrologer in Bangalore at 10-20 p.m. (IST) on 10-10-1978.

The question time would be:

10-20 p.m. (IST) on 10-10-1978 at Bangalore. Or, in other words, the chart is calculated for Bangalore at 10-20 p.m. (IST) on 10-10-1978.

9
How to Ask Questions

What is it that prompts one to approach an astrologer and seek guidance? It is, in most cases, a problem of intensity and gravity. Though the problem may have been there for some time, it is only at a particular instant of time that one is inadvertently driven to speak of it before an astrologer. This moment of time is important because it has given birth to a question. **The chart cast for this point of time carries with it the life of the question, what turn it will take and what end it will reach.**

The chart cast for a question carries with it just enough to answer that particular question. It is very important that only one question be asked at a time. Two or more questions coming in succession are like multiple births where the babies born rarely survive. The whole purpose of horary astrology is spoiled by asking more than one question at a time. One must always ask one question only at a time, clearly and briefly summing up the problem that needs a solution. Standard questions would be:

(1) When will I marry?

The chart for this question will answer if marriage is probable, of the likely time, the type of mate one may find and if the marriage will, by and large, be happy or not.

(2) When will I get a job?

This chart will answer when and the type of job and if it will be in the place of query or outside or abroad.

Instead, if you ask 'Will I get the job at the Aeronautical Laboratories or the Canara Bank?', you would be complicating matters for the astrologer. It would be hard to associate each of these concerns with the chart. The question simply framed would find in the chart whether the job has to do with accounts or engineering. This job may or may not be in the firms you have named. But the question 'Will I get a job in Canara Bank?' could be answered. Take care not to allow alternatives in the question.

(3) Will I marry X?

This question is possible if you are in love with X or your family is considering or negotiating an alliance with X's family. But again, if you reframe it as 'Will I marry X, Y or Z?' having 3 people in mind, you would not be helping either yourself or the astrologer in getting the right answer.

(4) Will I marry Z? Will I be able to get a deal through? Will I build my own house?

A spate of questions. The chart will not be able to give answers to a single one of your questions. Sometimes, people come to me to test if astrology works or if I am a good astrologer or just to while away time and ask frivolous questions. In such cases, I am neither polite nor patient but ask them to leave and not waste my time. Astrology is a serious subject and when ill-informed and impertinent people seek to make fun of it, be wary. Many times, when a person is not serious about a question, you will find the Ascendant to be on a cuspal degree. But sometimes, such an Ascendant is possible even in serious cases as you will, with experience, be able to gauge from the manner in which a person approaches you and recounts his woes to you.

10
Significations, Malefics and Benefics

In any question, the most important factor is the strength of the Ascendant, either by planets aspecting or Occupying it.

A benefic in or aspecting the Ascendant always bodes good and a favorable turn of events. Malefic aspects indicate the thing desired may never be or unfavorable results.

The natural benefics Mercury, Venus and Jupiter are always benefic.

The natural malefics Sun, Mars and Saturn are malefics unless rendering benefic by owning the Ascendant or the house to which the question refers.

Suppose, the question is 'Will I succeed in a particular venture?'

In Chart 18, the Ascendant is Aries occupied by Jupiter and aspected by Venus, both benefics, indicating success.

In Chart 19, the Ascendant is Libra aspected by a natural malefic Mars indicating defeat or loss.

In Chart 20, the Ascendant is Aquarius aspected by a natural malefic Saturn. But as the lord of the

	Lagna Jupiter		
	Chart 18 **Rasi**		
		Venus	

	Mars		
	Chart 19 **Rasi**		
		Lagna	

Lagna	**Chart 20** **Rasi**		
			Saturn

Ascendant, Saturn becomes a functional benefic indicating success. In any question, the Ascendant signifies the querent. The question must always relate

Significations, Malefics and Benefics

to one of the twelve houses in the chart. The lord of the house to which the question relates is called the significator. Take Chart 21 where Cancer is rising.

Jupiter	Mars	Venus	Mercury
Saturn	Chart 21 Rasi		Lagna Moon
Saturn			Sun
Jupiter	Mars	Venus	Mercury

Cancer and the Moon signify the person asking the question. In a question 'Will I get rich?' the 2nd lord the Sun becomes the significator.

In a question 'Will my missing brother return?' the 3rd lord Mercury is the significator.

In a question 'Will my mother recover her health?' the 4th lord Venus is the significator.

In a question 'Will my child pass her tests?' the 5th lord Mars is the significator.

In a question 'Will I win the court case?' the 6th lord Jupiter is the significator.

In a question 'When will I marry?' the 7th lord Saturn is the significator.

In a question 'Will I inherit a legacy?' the 8th lord Saturn becomes the significator.

In a question 'Will I go abroad?' the 9th lord Jupiter is the significator.

In a question 'Will I get a job?' the 10th lord Mars is the significator.

In a question 'Will my friend help me out?' the 11th lord Venus is the significator.

In a question 'Will I be imprisoned?' the 12th lord Mercury is the significator.

11
How to Read Aspects

Any Ithasala relationship between the Ascendant lord and the significator indicates that whatever the signification, good or bad, will be obtained by the querent.

In Chart 22, the question is 'Will I become rich?' The Ascendant and 2nd lords Venus and Mercury are in trinal houses in Ithasala indicating the native will come by money.

		Lagna 16°	
	Chart 22 Rasi		Mercury 8°
	Venus 10°		

In Chart 23, the question is 'Will I be imprisoned?' The Ascendant and 12th lord, Venus and Mars, are in Ithasala in the 12th house showing the querent will suffer confinement, arrest or imprisonment.

	Ven 12° Mars 15°	Lagna	
	Chart 23 Rasi		

In Chart 24, for the same question as in Chart 22, the Ascendant lord Saturn and significator Jupiter are not related in any manner. So the querent will get no riches.

	Saturn 15°	Jupiter 10°	
Lagna	Chart 24 Rasi		

In Chart 25, where the question is 'Will I suffer imprisonment?' there is no relationship between the Ascendant and 12th lords, the Sun and the Moon, so that the querent need have no fears of imprisonment.

Again, if the aspects are Ithasala or applying, it always denotes what will be in future. Separating aspects denote that the object of the question will not be fulfilled or it is something past.

How to Read Aspects

	Chart 25 **Rasi**		
Moon			Lagna
Sun		Venus	

In Chart 26, where the question is 'Will I marry X?' Jupiter signifies the querent and Mercury, X. Mercury is applying to a trine (120) of Jupiter. Mercury is in Ithasala with Jupiter. This indicates the querent will marry X.

Lagna			
	Chart 26 **Rasi**		
			Mercury 6°
Jupiter 10°			

In Chart 27, where the question is the same and also the significators, Mercury is moving away from the sextile (60) of Jupiter if Mercury be in Gemini. Suppose, Mercury is in Scorpio, then also, there is no aspect between him and Jupiter. In both these instances (Mercury in Gemini and Mercury in Scorpio in Chart 27), the querent and X will not marry and even if deeply in love with each other at the time of question, they may break up for some reason or the other.

Lagna			Mercury 25°
	Chart 27 Rasi		
			Jupiter 10°
	Mercury 25°		

Ithasala aspects can be sextile (60) or trine (120) or square (90), opposition (180) or conjunction (0). Ithasala aspects always denote success and a favorable outcome. The conjunction, sextile and trinal Ithasala aspects indicate that the object of the question will be fulfilled smoothly and easily with little or no effort.

In charts 28, 29, 30 where the question is 'Will I be successful in business', the Ascendant lord Saturn and 11th lord Mars are in Ithasala in sextile, conjunction and trine respectively, indicating that the querent will do well in business and easily attain prosperity.

		Mars 5°	
		Chart 28 Rasi	Saturn 10°
Lagna			

Chart 29 Rasi

Lagna	Chart 29 Rasi		Mars 5° Saturn 10°

Chart 30 Rasi

		Mars 5°	
Lagna	Chart 30 Rasi		
			Saturn 10°

Where the Ithasala aspects are hostile, delay and opposition are indicated and with much effort and perseverance, the object may still be attained.

Chart 31 Rasi

		Mars 5°	
Lagna	Chart 31 Rasi		Saturn 10°

In Chart 31, for the same question 'Will I prosper in business', the Ascendant and 11th lords are in square Ithasala. The querent will find himself against heavy odds, his goods will not sell easily and the whole venture may prove gloomy. But inspite of all this, if the querent is prepared to do his utmost and not give up, success will come to him slowly but surely.

12

The Role of the Moon and the Eleventh House

The Moon is a very important factor in horary astrology. The Moon in Ithasala with any planet indicates the significations of its lordship will come about.

In Chart 32, the Moon is in Ithasala with the Ascendant and 4th lord in the 5th indicating success in examinations and competitive tests (ruled by 4th lord Mercury), and as 2nd lord applying to Ascendant lord, gain of money.

			Lagna
	Chart 32		
	Rasi		Moon 5°
		Mercury 10°	

In any question, the Moon in favorable Ithasala aspect to the significator emphasizes, hastens, expedites the fulfilment of the querent's wishes.

In Chart 33, in a question 'Shall I invest in certain shares', the 5th lord Mercury (ruling shares, speculation) applies to the Ascendant lord Venus. The aspect is semi-sextile and not feeble. But the Moon applies both to the 5th and 11th lords strengthening the chart and emphasizing the success of making the investment.

Venus 20°		Lagna	
Mercury 11°	**Chart 33** **Rasi**		
	Moon 8°		

If the Moon was not to apply, the investment would fetch profits, but after a delayed period and also not of a sizeable amount.

The natural nature of the planets to whom the Moon applies also indicates the immediate turn of events, whatever the final outcome.

		Moon 3°	
	Chart 34 **Rasi**		
			Venus 5°

In Chart 34, the Moon applies to Venus, a benefic expansive planet so that the querent may expect a happy and bright phase following the question, irrespective of the final result being good or bad.

In Chart 35, whatever the question or final result, the period immediately following the question may be marked by utter despondency and despair, if the planet is Saturn. If Mars, the querent may quarrel and meet with much hostility and opposition. If both Mars and Saturn, the querent will just about lose all hope in his fond desire, meet with the greatest impediments but the final outcome will depend upon the Ascendant and significator.

		Moon	
	Chart 35 Rasi		Mars or Saturn

The Moon's application is very important and where it is not present, delay or a state of seeming hopelessness may prevail.

In Chart 36, the Ascendant is Aries and Ascendant lord Mars is in the 4th in debilitation. The Moon is exalted in the 2nd. The Moon applies to Mars and we see Mars, though Ascendant lord is also the 8th lord. The Ascendant is weak. We may safely conclude the querent's question will find a favorable answer but the querent himself may suddenly die before the object of the question is fulfilled. This is because the Moon is strongly and favorably disposed with the reference to Ascendant lord and the 8th lord who is at the same time a malefic made worse by retrogression and debilitation.

	Lagna 0° 54	Moon 15°	
	Chart 36 Rasi		Mars (R) 19°

Besides what we have already seen, the 11th house is very important in judging the final outcome of any issue. The eleventh house rules gains primarily. Gains or *labha* signify profits or the advantageous outcome of a situation. As such, the 11th house is of very great importance in finding out if something hoped or worked for will fructify.

In Chart 37, whatever the query the answer would be for a favorable result. Whether it is 'Will a particular party win the election?' or 'Will I marry well?' or 'Will I be able to put a deal through?' or any other question, the answer would invariably be a 'yes'. Yes, the party will win the elections, you will marry well, or you will be able to get the deal through most advantageously. The Lagna lord Venus is in Ithasala with Jupiter, the 11th lord. It is immaterial that Venus is exalted although his dignity will only make it easier for the querent to obtain fulfilment of

The Role of the Moon and the Eleventh House

his wishes. More so, the Lagna lord Venus being in the 11th house or house of gains.

Venus 6°	Jupiter 10°	Lagna	
	Chart 37 Rasi		

In Charts 38 and 39, where the same two planets figure, the outcome would still be favorable, notwithstanding the hostile and friendly Ithasala Yogas respectively. In Chart 38, Ascendant lord is in the 6th but in own sign and 11th lord Jupiter is in his sign of debility. This would delay matters, raise hurdles but also endow the native with sufficient persistence and perseverance to earn what he wants which he will finally get. In Chart 39, both are debilitated but in trine in Ithasala, so that success will come easier than in the preceding case. In this instance, the querent

		Lagna	
	Chart 38 Rasi		
Jupiter 20°			
		Venus 8°	

may stoop to slightly unfair means to gain his ends, as the two planets are in debility.

		Lagna	
	Chart 39 Rasi		
Jupiter 20°			
			Venus 10°

The importance of the Ascendant lord in Ithasala with the 11th lord can never be under-rated. In any chart, no matter what the malefic and negative influences, this particular Ithasala has in it the power to give the querent realization of his hopes, the degree of success being qualified by the malefic factors.

For instance, in Chart 40, the question 'Will I marry the girl I love', the significators would seem to be Jupiter and 7th lord Mercury. The Ascendant is aspected by an ill-placed Mars who is also retrograde. This, in itself, is not a very good factor. The Ascendant lord is in the 4th trining 7th lord Mercury but it is not an Ithasala. The Moon is weak, being New, and although sextile both significators, there is no Ithasala Yoga. Inspite of tremendous opposition, the querent succeeded in marrying his sweetheart. How did this happen? The strength of the Ascendant lord Jupiter who is in the 4th in his own sign and stationery shows a positive answer. Here, since it is a case of being in love, Mars as 5th lord ruling emotions become the significator, not the 7th lord Mercury as in an arranged proposal. Mars showing the girl he is in love with as a faster planet with less longitude is moving backwards towards the slower Jupiter with greater longitude showing the two will marry.

Jupiter 20° (Stationary)	Ketu 18°		Mars (R) 10°
	Chart 40 Rasi		Saturn 20°
Sun 28° Moon 27°			
Lagna 7°	Mercury 28°	Venus 11° Rahu 18°	

Planets in conjunction with the Ascendant lord indicate the present, those in Ithasala, the future, while those in Easarapha, the past.

In Chart 41, the Ascendant lord Mars is in the 6th with 8th lord Mercury indicating the querent is passing through a very frustrating period and with health also causing problems.

	Mercury 18° Mars 20°		Venus 22°
Moon 10°	Chart 41 Rasi		Saturn 25°
	Lagna		

Mars, the Ascendant lord, is in Ithasala with 9th lord Moon as well as Mercury, 11th lord, indicating that things will brighten up very soon and it is not unlikely the native may come by sufficient money or opportunities (11th lord Mercury) to take him abroad (9th lord Moon). This in all probability for reasons of further education (Moon, the 9th lord, is in the 4th house), since Mars is also in Ithasala with Saturn, the 4th lord in the 9th.

The 7th lord Venus has no Ithasala with Mars but is in Easarapha, although in a different sign. The frustration and misery of the past months could be due to an engagement having broken up or a romantic friendship (Venus as Karaka for love) having come to an unhappy end.

13
Some Exceptions

Although the opposition is an indication of adverse or negative results, there is an exception when the Lagna comes under the 7th house aspect of a planet.

In Chart 42, the Ascendant is aspected by Jupiter. The aspect is an opposition but Jupiter being a benefic, his aspect is desirable and indicates success.

	Lagna 10°		
	Chart 42		
	Rasi		
		Jupiter 6°	

In Chart 43, the Ascendant Aries is aspected by Mars, a malefic. But Mars is the Lagna lord and his aspect indicates a positive outcome.

In Chart 44, Saturn aspecting the Lagna is a natural malefic and not the Lagna lord either, and the aspect can only give failure or negative results.

In the question 'Will I marry a certain girl?' in Chart 45 at 13h.00m. (IST) on 22-8-1976 at Bangalore,

	Lagna 12°		
	Chart 43 **Rasi**		
	Mars 15°		

Lagna 7°			
	Chart 44 **Rasi**		
			Saturn 10°

the Ascendant is aspected by a benefic Jupiter but the significators Mars and Venus have no aspect. This would mean the querent would, no doubt, marry but not the girl he has in mind. The lack of aspect between the two significators indicates nothing will come out of the proposal. Jupiter's aspect indicates he will find some other girl for a bride who will be a devoted wife. Mars, the Ascendant lord, in Ithasala with the 11th lord would fetch a wife from a good family. Jupiter in the 7th will keep the marriage happy.

If Saturn, instead, were to occupy the 7th in Taurus, the querent would be condemned to a life of bachelorhood, not being able to marry either the proposal before him or even any other.

Some Exceptions

	Ketu 14° 47	Jupiter 7° 50	Moon 26° 50
	Chart 45 **Rasi**		Saturn 17° 31
			Sun 7° 20 Venus 25°
	Lagna 14° 40	Rahu 14° 47	Mercury 4° 45 Mars 6° 50

In Chart 40, which we have already discussed once before, we shall look into Mars' aspect on Lagna.

Mars aspects Lagna powerfully from the 7th as a malefic. This should not allow the marriage to take place. But it has already occurred. This is because Mars is the significator and his aspect on the Lagna becomes supportive. Jupiter is very powerful being stationary in the 4th in his own sign. So Jupiter's static state against Mars' retrograde state led to severe conflict and tremendous tension and confusion. Mars in the 7th will create discord and problems in married life, which, in turn, will resolve themselves in the strong position of Jupiter in the 4th.

3-31 p.m. (IST) on 13-7-1976 at Bangalore. Is there any danger to longevity or will I die soon? (Chart 46)

In Chart 46, the querent had been told by a doctor that he was going to die very soon within the next few months. The querent was greatly alarmed by this medical prediction. His mother thought astrological guidance could help him.

			Moon 26° 26' Sun 12°25'
	Ketu 16° 53'	Jupiter 2°23'	
	Chart 46 Rasi		Venus 6° 59' Saturn 12° 425'
Moon 22° 54'			Mars 12° 4'
	Lagna 12° 48'	Rahu 16° 59'	

Jupiter is in opposition to Lagna and Mars is squaring Lagna. Jupiter is a benefic, Mars is the Ascendant lord and together indicate that the querent has a long life and there is no need to drive himself crazy over the doctor's prediction.

Planets in opposition may give adverse results but planets in the 7th or 10th house from the Lagna do not necessarily imply evil. Here, the aspects are reckoned according to the Parasari system where all planets aspect the 7th house from the one they occupy.

Mars and Saturn in addition have special aspects. The 4th or 7th house aspect of Mars on the Ascendant as its lord is not adverse.

The 7th house aspect of Venus, Mercury and Jupiter is beneficial.

The 10th house aspect of Saturn as Lagna lord on the Lagna is not harmful.

But Mars and Saturn cause negative results by these same aspects if they do not happen to be Lagna lords or significators.

14
Timing Events

We now come to the important task of timing events. As in natal astrology, this is one of the hardest and most challenging jobs of an astrologer. It is a relatively easy thing to say what will happen, but as to when, well that is totally different. It requires all the skill and patience you can command.

Ancient works on astrology have given time-periods over which planets hold sway:

Sun	—	half a year or 6 months
Moon	—	a Muhurtha or 48 minutes
Mars	—	one day
Mercury	—	two months
Jupiter	—	one month
Venus	—	15 days
Saturn	—	one year

The aspect of Saturn on the Ascendant, or significator or the Moon generally indicates undue delay. The Moon in the 6th, the 8th or the 12th and also in the 7th, points to obstacles of one sort or the other that will hinder progress of the issue and consequently delay the matter.

Moveable signs when involved indicate fairly fast results. Fixed signs show delay and a slow pace. Common signs show fairly fast results.

Sometimes, moveable signs indicate days, common signs, weeks and fixed signs, months. Planets in Kendras (1, 4, 7, 10) give results in days, planets in Panaparas (2, 5, 8, 11) show results in weeks while those in Apoklimas or cadent houses (3, 6, 9, 12) rule months.

Another method is to push off the result by one year if the Moon is in the 6th or the 8th, or if Saturn aspects the Ascendant, significator or significant.

Sometimes, an event can be indicated when Jupiter trines or passes the significator in transit or forms a favorable aspect with the Ascendant or the Moon. If the event in issue is a death or unhappy event, it can be anticipated fairly accurately by the transits of Saturn over sensitive areas of the chart. Generally, the period when the significators come to an exact aspect can be taken to time the event in question.

The number of degrees between the planets can be taken to determine the period when the event they signify may occur.

11-40 a.m. (IST) on 7-9-1977 at Bangalore (Chart 47)

Will my missing son return?

Here in Chart 47, the question relates to the son of the querent who had left home in a huff after an altercation. The Lagna and 5th lord Mars and Jupiter are in conjunction with the Moon. Since both significators are in Ithasala with the Moon and the

Moon and Mars are separated by slightly over a degree, the son could be expected to return within a day. He came back on the 8th morning round 11-30.

			Moon 10° 25' Jupiter 10° 37' Mars 11°43'
Ketu 24° 35'			
	\multicolumn{2}{c}{Chart 47 Rasi}	Venus 19° 21'
			Saturn 1° 21' Mercury (R) 18° 34' Sun 22° 24'
	Lagna 11° 39'		Rahu 24° 35'

If in moveable signs or Kendras, as many days as the degrees between the two will indicate the date of the event. Fixed and common signs will respectively, denote as many months or years.

It would not be sensible to give exact dates. It would be better to give a range of weeks or months for the occurrence of the event. In all cases, you must go by your own skill adapting the general principles to each individual chart as a whole.

The Moon's Ithasala with both Ascendant lord and significator generally indicates quick results.

12-40 p.m. on 2-7-1978 at Bangalore.

Do I have any chances of foreign travel? (Chart 48)

Ketu 8° 42'		Moon 13° 45'	Sun 17° 57' Jupiter 24° 20'
	\multicolumn{2}{c	}{**Chart 48** **Rasi**}	Mercury 9° Venus 29° 10'
			Saturn 5° 28'
	Lagna 11° 39'		Rahu 8° 42' Lagna 20° 16'

In Chart 48, the Lagna lord and 9th lord Mercury and Venus are in Ithasala in the 11th. The Moon, as 11th lord as well, is in exaltation and in Ithasala with 9th lord Venus. Venus and the Moon are in exchange of signs making the chart very strong to confer foreign travel. Within 4 months in October 1978, the querent left India for the United States. At the time of question, the querent had no plans nor was there any other indication for foreign travel. He only had dreams. As soon as he was told of the bright chances that were there astrologically, he walked into the Visa Office and in no time plans were made and finalised.

7-15 p.m. (IST) on 15-1-1975 at Bangalore.

When will I get married? (Chart 49)

		Ketu 15° 46'	Saturn (R) 22° 38'
Jupiter 23° 56' Moon 9° 20'	**Chart 49** **Rasi**		Lagna 16° 52'
Venus 18° 53' Mercury 17° 45' Sun 2° 39'			
Mars 3° 31'	Rahu 15° 46'		

In Chart 49, benefics Venus and Mercury are aspecting the Ascendant. The significators Moon and Saturn are in Ithasala but the Moon is in the 8th, a Dustana. Marriage came nearly a year later in December 1975.

The Sun's change of sign or the change of motion of a planet from direct to retrograde motion or vice-versa can also be effectively used to time an event fairly successfully.

2-00 p.m. (IST) on 24-1-1975 at 13° N, 77° E 35'.

Will I find the missing file containing important papers?

In Chart 50, the Ascendant rules the querent and the 11th house, the object of query, namely, documents. The Lagna and 11th lord are in Ithasala. The 11th lord is in Aquarius, an airy sign with Venus and Mercury. Venus indicates bedrooms while Mercury rules book-

		Moon 26° 50' Lagna 11° 44' Ketu 15° 18'	Saturn (R) 21° 56'
Jupiter 25° 36' Mercury 0° 10' Venus 0° 15'	\multicolumn{2}{c|}{Chart 50 Rasi}	
Sun 11° 19'			
Mars 9° 50'	Rahu 15° 18'		

cases, shelves, filing cabinets and similar places. The sign being airy, it was surmised, the file would be at a height in one of the bedrooms on top of a book-shelf. The Sun was due to change signs from Capricorn to Aquarius on February 13, 1975 which was given as the date when the file would be found. A search was made immediately following the prediction in all the bedrooms that had book-cases or papers in them with no success. On the 14th morning, while trying to bring down a stack of old newspapers kept on top of a Godrej bureau containing files and papers, the whole lot slipped and came down. The lost file slid out through one of these newspapers. Nobody could guess how the file got there in the first place, but everyone was relieved it had been safe all along.

15
Bhava, Combustion, Nodes and Retrogression

The Bhava chart is a very important chart in answering questions. The Bhava chart we use is based on the Equal House Division System which takes 15° on either side of the Ascendant as constituting the first Bhava.

			Lagna 25°
	Chart 51		
Saturn 2°	**Rasi**		
Jupiter 2°			

In Chart 51, the Lagna extends from 10° Gemini to 10° Cancer, 15° on either side of the Lagna degree. Jupiter in 4° Sagittarius does not aspect the Lagna, being in the 6th Bhava actually. Saturn in 2° Capricorn will aspect the Lagna from the 7th Bhava.

This would mean an unfavourable result or failure of the object the querent has in mind, notwithstanding Jupiter in the 7th sign.

		Jupiter 18°	
	Chart 52		Saturn 29°
Lagna 2°	**Rasi**		

In Chart 52, the query relates to whether the querent would be able to extend his stay in India.

The Lagna is aspected by Saturn, Lagna lord, and Jupiter, a benefic but in the Bhava chart, Jupiter moves into the 6th Bhava and Saturn to the 8th Bhava, so that the answer would invariably be negative.

Retrogression

Retrograde planets are a little tricky of interpretation. Experience has shown that natural benefics such as Mercury, Venus and Jupiter remain benefic while the malefics Mars and Saturn, even if Lagna lords or significators, become troublesome.

In Chart 53, the question is whether 'I will marry a certain person?'. Jupiter aspects Lagna. So does Lagna lord Saturn and also a malefic Mars. This would normally indicate an answer in the affirmative. In the case in issue, the retrogression of the malefics Mars and Saturn literally exploded the dreams of the querent by a cruel trick of fate. Both are retrograde and easily could overpower Jupiter's benefic aspect.

Benefic planets when retrograde continue to be benefic, although they may make the process of achieving the object in view a little erratic or evasive.

		Moon 9° 50'	Jupiter (R) 6° 35'
Lagna 3° 11'	**Chart 53** **Rasi**		Mars (R) 10° 40'
Sun 6° 34' Venus 5° 9'			Saturn (R) 8° 8'
Mercury 14° 20'			Rahu 17° 30'

Nodes

Rahu and Ketu can be ignored safely for the greater part of our study. Only the Moon's aspect to either Node can indicate the state of mind the querent will pass through. The Moon's conjunction with Rahu or Ketu will indicate confusion and despondency.

If any significator (when indicating persons) is with Rahu, it can be implied to mean the person may try to deceive or fool the querent. But if the chart is strongly indicative of success, the querent will be none the worse for all the deceit employed against him.

Combustion

Where the Sun is one of the significators or the lord of Lagna, his association with another planet and the other's consequent combustion will not at all affect the chart. Where the Sun is neither the significator nor the Ascendant lord, combustion will destroy the signification, the degree depending upon the closeness of the Sun and the planet.

Mercury and Venus suffer no combustion in Prasna charts.

Jupiter, Mars and Saturn lose their power to confer their significations if combust.

8 a.m. (IST) on 29-7-1977 at Madras. (Chart 54)

Ketu 26° 44'		Mars 15° 18'	Venus 2° 23' Jupiter (R) 3° 43'
	\multicolumn{2}{c|}{Chart 54 Rasi}	Sun 13° 47' Saturn 26° 23'
			Mercury 8° 50' Lagna 12° 49'
Moon 25° 18'			Rahu 26° 44'

In Chart 54, the worried management of an industrial concern had to resort to lock-out of the workers following union trouble.

The Ascendant lord Sun and 6th lord Saturn are the planets involved in Ithasala Yoga in the 12th house. Lagna has benefic Mercury. The lock-out was lifted on 17th August 1977 following a compromise between the workers and the management. Saturn, even if combust, would not have made a big difference since the Sun (who causes combustion) is one of the significators.

16
Practical Illustrations

We have so far seen how to come to a result merely by the benefic or malefic aspects figuring certain important factors such as the Ascendant, its lord, the Moon and the 11th lord.

Benefic aspects on the Ascendant and its lord indicate a happy state of affairs may be expected. Malefic aspects indicate danger of death, illness, accidents, loss of happiness and unfavorable trends in general.

Consider the Ascendant, its lord, the Moon and aspects these receive. If the Ascendant lord aspects the Ascendant, or if benefics aspect the Ascendant or the Ascendant lord, or if the Ascendant and 11th lords are favorably disposed, predict the querent's luck will take a turn for the better.

In Chart 55, the Ascendant is Scorpio aspected by its lord Mars and two natural benefics, Venus and Jupiter. Mars being in the 6th house (though in 7th sign) indicates the state of the native was one of despair at the time of question. The 6th rules disease and debts, both of which were troubling the querent which he later confirmed as the cause for his unhappy state of mind.

4-20 p.m., IST, on 7-7-1977 at 13° N, 77° 30' E.

Will my future be any better? A most depressing phase since the last two years. (Chart 55)

Ketu 27° 51' Moon 14° 50'		Mars 3° 43' Venus 0° 37' Jupiter 29° 6'	Sun 23° 8'
	Chart 55 **Rasi**		Mercury 1° 50' Saturn 23° 44'
	Ascdt 16° 08'		Rahu 27° 51'

We see the Moon applies first to Ketu, a Node, by no means a benefic, indicating things would continue to be bad for some more time.

The aspect of two benefics on the Ascendant indicates a relatively better phase is soon due, that is, a period of luck will begin shortly.

The Ascendant lord Mars is in Ithasala with Jupiter — 2nd and 5th lord as well as the Sun — the 10th lord. So, financially his state would improve considerably through his securing a good job and he would also go abroad in all likelihood. The job would have to do with magnificent abodes and some business connected with catering since Lagna lord Mars was in Taurus (ruling places of eating, ease and luxury) with Venus (ruling glamour, good things of life, enjoyment) and Jupiter (palatial abodes and as 5th lord, investment or business). The querent confirmed he had applied for and was hopeful of getting a job in a five-star hotel in a major city of India. A five-star hotel, as everyone knows, is the last word in good living and it is a business of catering and providing abodes or lodging.

It was also indicated the querent would not remain in that job for long (10th lord Sun in the 8th to whom Lagna lord Mars applies indicating job-dissatisfaction and frustration), but would seek his fortune abroad since the 9th lord and Lagna lord, the Moon and Mars, apply to the 3d lord Saturn ,placed in the 9th (in Ithasala with the 11th lord Mercury).

All of which the querent confirmed a few months later. He had got the job in the hotel in Bombay but found he did not like it there. He had then, with the aid of a friend, gone to the Middle East where he is now quite happy.

In Chart 56, the Ascendant is Aries. The Ascendant lord Mars is in the 4th debilitated and retrograde. He is also the 8th lord. Neither the Ascendant nor Mars receives any benefic aspects. The Moon applies to Mars as Lagna lord and 8th lord linking the querent with death. The querent can, therefore, have little hope for recovery but must prepare for death shortly. Although Mars to whom the Moon applies is the Ascendant lord, we must note the fact of the extreme maleficence he picks up by a combination of debility and retrogression.

The querent collapsed 3 days later on New Year's eve following a massive heart attack.

1-25 p.m., 28-12-1977, at 13° N, 77° E 30'.

My health has been very bad. Will it improve? (Chart 56)

Ketu 18° 39'	Lagna 5° 14'		Jupiter 8° 16'
Moon 10°			Moon 14° 58' Mars 17° 50'
	Chart 56 Rasi		Saturn 8° 10'
Sun 14° Venus 8° Mercury 0° 04'			Rahu 18° 39'

7-05 a.m. (IST) on 13-6-1975 at 13° N, 77° E 30.

Will the Prime Minister Mrs. Indira Gandhi remain in power or go? (Chart 57)

Jupiter 26° 50' Mars 24° 48'		Ketu 7° 54' Mercury (R) 25° 57' Sun 29°	Lagna 13° Saturn 26°
			Moon 11° Venus 14°
	Chart 57 Rasi		

Practical Illustrations 93

This question was asked just before the *Emergency* was clamped in India. People had begun to distrust the then Prime Minister Mrs. Indira Gandhi and her tactics. She had created resentment amongst the people by her authoritarian methods of ruling the country. Note the Ascendant in Chart 57 is occupied by a malefic Saturn and aspected by another malefic Mars. Ascendant lord Mercury is in the 12th, the house of loss. These denote she will lose power. The Moon applies to Venus indicating a favorable trend for her in the immediate future. The 10th lord is in the 10th in Ithasala with the 6th and 11th lord Mars and aspected exactly by Saturn by an hostile aspect or square. The conclusion you can draw, therefore, is a turn of events to make things easy for her, followed by a consolidation of her position. But Saturn in the Ascendant and Mercury in the 12th indicate the gains will not remain for long and she must step down finally.

Soon after in July 1975, came the *Emergency* followed by the 19 months of authoritarian rule. In March 1977, the elections of the Lok Sabha were announced. The Prime Minister who had considered herself indispensable to the country was rejected by her own constituency by the popular vote. She had to step down from power after a reign of nearly 11 years.

You will see the Ascendant comes under only unfavorable aspects. So does the Ascendant lord Mercury.

1-43 p.m. (IST) on 14-7-1976 at Bangalore. When will I get a job? (Chart 58)

	Ketu 16° 51'	Jupiter 2° 11'	Mercury 28° 23' Sun 29° 58'
Moon 4° 37'		Chart 58 Rasi	Venus 7° 08' Saturn 12° 32'
			Mars 12° 23'
		Rahu 16° 51' Lagna 18° 55'	

This question came from a young man who was forced to give up his job of 10 years in a bank following much unpleasantness with the staff and customers alike.

The Ascendant lord Venus (Chart 58) is in the 10th in Ithasala with 4th and 5th lord Saturn. The 10th lord Moon signifying job (occupation) is in Ithasala with both Venus and Saturn. Venus as Lagna lord in the 10th indicates self-employment. Saturn as 4th lord indicates vehicles. The querent will, therefore, find an occupation of an independent nature and not a job in the sense of service. Saturn is with Lagna lord indicating delay while the Ithasala of the Moon with Lagna lord must hasten matters at least to a degree. It would, therefore, be at least 8-12 months before he would find himself employed again. The Moon as 10th lord and Venus in Cancer are indicative of running some transport for public utility. Venus is in Ithasala to Mars, 2nd lord in the 11th, indicating earnings.

In May 1977, exactly 10 months later, the querent bought an autorickshaw and began to ply it for hire in Bangalore. He was soon earning well enough to maintain himself in comfort.

If we apply the keys in Chapter 2, the Ascendant is Libra indicating "tall and elegant with slim bodies, pimpled........", while referring to Chapter 5, Venus in Cancer gives "fleshy body of medium height, dark thick hair", while Saturn in Cancer shows one with "short, ill-formed stature, dark complexion, grizzly hair. Eyes are neurotic and malicious looking".

Venus and Libra are primary factors being Lagna lord and Lagna respectively in describing the native. Venus associates with Saturn partaking some of his characteristics.

The querent was fleshy, good-looking, fairly tall with dark thick grizzly hair and nuerotic eyes.

2-55 p.m. on 17-6-1976 at Bangalore.

Will I marry the girl I am engaged to? (Chart 59)

The Lagna in Chart 59 is aspected by Jupiter which is, however, powerless, Jupiter having shifted to the 8th house. Lagna and 7th lord Venus and Mars are in Ithasala. Venus ruling Lagna and Mars ruling 7th house as the significators and the Sun as 11th lord are in Ithasala. The Moon is in Ithasala with 7th lord Mars, Saturn is with 7th lord Mars and also aspects the 7th by his 10th house aspect. This indicates delay

	Ketu 18° 20' Jupiter 27° 15'	Mercury 11° 20'	Venus 4° 31' Sun 4° 15'
Moon 9° 59'		**Chart 59** **Rasi**	Saturn 9° 17' Mars 26° 16'
		Lagna 10° 42' Rahu 18°	

by at least 2 years but the Ithasala Yogas will see to it that the couple will eventually marry.

The querent had been engaged to a particular girl but the marriage itself was being indefinitely postponed. The girl's father was away in Burma for many years where, her mother feared, he had another family. She believed she could use the girl's marriage as a handle to bring her husband back to her at least for a while. So, she thought, if she delayed the marriage, he would have a reason to come back.

Anyway, whatever the girl's mother's problems, the querent was despondent about the whole thing. In September 1978, the querent married his fiancee exactly 2 years and 3 months from the date of question.

The Lagna in Chart 60 is aspected by malefic retrograde Saturn. The significators Venus and Mars are in opposition, the 7th lord Mars being retrograde.

2-10 p.m. (IST) on 23-1-1978 at Bangalore.

Will I marry the man I love? (Chart 60)

Ketu 17° 14'		Lagna 14° 50'	Jupiter (R) 5° 10'
	Chart 60 Rasi		Moon 0° 10' Mars (R) 9° 37'
Venus 12° 20' Sun 10° 51'			Saturn (R) 8° 8'
Mercury 20°			Rahu 17° 14'

The Moon feebly applies to Mars and Saturn respectively.

This question came from a young working girl who had been in love with a colleague for nearly 3 years. The colleague had promised to marry her. He had suddenly refused to marry saying his parents would never agree to their marriage. The girl was in a very disturbed state of mind.

Mars is retrograde indicating the man had backed out. Retrograde Saturn, a powerful malefic, aspects the Ascendant. The opposition between Mars and Venus is also Easarpha indicating she will not marry him. Taking the 5th lord as significator also leads to the same conclusion.

4-00 p.m. (IST) on 25-11-1977 at Bangalore.

Should I go abroad and accept a scholarship for further studies? (Chart 61)

Ketu 20° 21'	Lagna 12° 31'	Moon 7° 45'	Jupiter (R) 12° 23'
	\multicolumn{2}{c	}{**Chart 61** **Rasi**}	Mars 17° 40'
			Saturn 8° 12'
Mercury 0° 45'	Sun 11°	Venus 17° 15'	Rahu 20° 21'

The query came from an enterprising young man who was managing the family business. He had received a very attractive offer for study abroad. He was worried if the family business would suffer if he accepted the offer and could not decide what to do.

A benefic aspect in the Ascendant is always welcome and says "Go ahead". Venus in Chart 61 aspects the Ascendant from his Moolatrikona sign. The Ascendant lord Mars is in the 4th house (education) in Ithasala with an exalted Moon who happens to be the 4th lord himself indicating not only success but also distinction in studies contemplated. The Moon is also in Ithasala with Jupiter who is the 9th lord ruling foreign travel as well as the 12th lord ruling foreign residence. These several Yogas indicate travel abroad and a happy successful time there.

What about the family business?

The 12th being the 11th from the 2nd rules family business. The 12th lord Jupiter is in Ithasala with an exalted Moon and is in opposition to 3rd and 6th lord Mercury. Mercury occupying a cusp is weak and the two planets being in Parivartana give results as if Jupiter were in the 9th in semi-sextile Ithasala with the Moon which indicates the business will take care of itself with initial problems between the remaining brothers (Mercury as 3rd lord) handling it. All the aspects are favorable except Saturn aspecting the Moon. This would mean a slight delay but the predominating influences being benefic, the querent would leave India in about 3 months' time. In March 1978 the querent left for England for further studies.

9-05 a.m. on 25-11-1975 at Bangalore.

Will I pass my B.Com. examination? (Chart 62)

Jupiter 23° 5'	Ketu 29° 9'		Mars (R) 7° 59' Lagna 29° 21'
	Chart 62 Rasi		Saturn (R) 10° 50'
			Moon 20° 19'
	Sun 11° 41' Mercury 8° 45'	Rahu 29° 9'	Venus 25° 4'

In Chart 62, Mars is in the Ascendant but luckily shifts to the 12th Bhava. The Ascendant lord Mercury is in the 6th. The 4th is occupied by a benefic Venus and aspected by another benefic Jupiter indicating success. But Mercury being in the 6th as the 4th lord and Lagna point being hemmed in between 2 malefics longitudinally would indicate only a passable performance.

The results showed the querent as having passed in the III class.

8-30 a.m. (IST) on 19-4-1975 at Bangalore.

Will the key-bunch be found (not sure whether lost or misplaced)? (Chart 63)

Jupiter 15° 27'	Sun 6° 20' Mercury 6° 28'	Ketu 10° 47' Lagna 12° 58' Venus 14°	Saturn 21° 2'
Mars 13° 26'		Chart 63 Rasi	Moon 5° 28'
	Rahu 10° 47'		

In Chart 63, the Ascendant and its lord as always signify the querent. The key-bunch is ruled by the 2nd house and its lord coming under 'possessions'.

The Ascendant is occupied by a benefic and Ascendant lord Venus. The 2nd lord Mercury is in conjunction with the 4th lord Sun.

The keys must, therefore, be found in or about their usual place and somewhere within the house (Sun 4th lord) in some bed (12th house) or Venus Lagna lord in the fixed Lagna increases the chances of the lost object being where it should be.

The keys were found in a week's time under the mattress on the cot. The presence of strong Venus in Taurus indicates places such as bedrooms, beds, etc.

The keys were found on the 23rd April when Mercury and Venus were in exact sextile.

6-50 p.m. on 4-11-1975 at Bangalore.

Will I get a doctorate degree? (Chart 64)

Jupiter (R) 24° 53'	Lagna 2° 21'	Ketu 0° 13'	Mars 10° 34'
	Chart 64 Rasi		Saturn 10° 49'
	Rahu 0° 13' Moon 12° 8'	Mercury 4° 56' Sun 19° 23'	Venus 2° 51'

In Chart 64, the Ascendant is aspected by a benefic Mercury, significator of learning.

The 11th rules honours, awards, distinction and recognition.

The Lagna is aspected by 11th lord Saturn with whom the Lagna lord Mars is in Ithasala. The Moon is in Ithasala with Jupiter, a benefic. The Moon is ruler of the 4th having to do with education. Mercury is the Karaka of academic bodies and learning and Saturn, the 11th lord, is in the 4th indicating gain of an academic distinction from a body or institution of learning. Mars and Saturn conjoined in Cancer in May 1976 which was indicated as the period by when the querent would be conferred a doctorate by an Indian university.

In June 1976, a university in North India conferred the honorary doctorate of "Doctor of Letters" on the querent at its annual convocation.

11-38 a.m. (IST) on 14-12-1976 at Bangalore.

Will I get a national award in 1977 ? (Chart 65)

	Ketu 8° 45'	Jupiter 0° 50'	
Lagna 15° 41'	Chart 65 Rasi		Saturn (R) 24° 34'
Venus 13° 29'			Moon 28° 6'
Mercury 19° 12' Sun 0° 18'	Mars 24° 47'	Rahu 8° 45'	

This question was asked by a noted exponent of classical music. He had just about received every award and distinction that was available in the country and his only desire was to get the Padma Vibhushan.

In Chart 65, the Ascendant is Aquarius with its lord Saturn in the 6th. There are no benefic aspects on the Ascendant. The 11th lord is in the 5th but very feeble being in a cuspal degree. Only malefic Mars aspects the Ascendant. The Moon has no Ithasala with any planet. It was unlikely, therefore, he would get the award he coveted.

In July 1977, the Government of India banned all awards such as the Padmashri, the Padma Bhushan, the Padma Vibhushan and the Bharat Ratna.

10 a.m. (IST) on 11-1-1978 at Bangalore.

Will I win the elections (M.L.A.) in Karnataka on a Congress (Deve Gowda) ticket? (Chart 66)

Practical Illustrations

Ketu 17° 55'			Jupiter (R) 6° 27'
Lagna 20° 7'	**Chart 66** **Rasi**		Mars 13° 40'
Moon 26° 51'			Saturn (R) 8° 36'
Sun 28° 40' Venus 25° 50' Mercury 4° 7'			Rahu 17° 55'

In Chart 66, the 10th House represents office, post, status and influence. If the querent should win, she would become a member of the Legislative Assembly which would give her considerable influence. As such, the 10th lord Mars becomes significator. Saturn and Mars as Lagna and the 10th lords have no aspect and both are retrograde. The Moon is not in aspect with either. Jupiter does aspect the Ascendant but from a Bhava-cusp and has to reckon with aspect of Saturn (R). It was indicated the querent would have difficulty in getting the ticket itself from the party, let alone win the elections. The querent's name appeared in the preliminary lists of contestants but was absent in the final list. She could not contest the elections at all.

6-28 p.m. (IST) on 26-3-1975 at Bangalore.

Will my missing brother return? (Chart 67)

The querent's brother had left home following an altercation with the parents. In Chart 67, Mars signifying the missing brother is exalted showing how the brother was hot-headed and acted on impulse. Mercury signifies the querent. The two are not in Ithasala but benefic Jupiter aspects the Ascendant. The Moon, by himself, and also as the 11th lord is in Ithasala with both significators, Mars and Mercury.

Jupiter 9° 55'	Venus 15° 59'	Ketu 12° 3'	Saturn 20° 01'
Mercury 22° 44'	Chart 67 Rasi		
Moon 25° 35'			
	Rahu 12° 3'		Moon 0° 24' Lagna 12° 7'

A common sign rising and the significator Mars exalted in a moveable sign indicates the brother will regain self-control soon and come back home of his own accord by about the time the Moon and Mars from an exact trine, that is, in two days' time. The brother returned on the 27th evening.

A certain title on a technical subject written by an authority on the subject published by a publisher of moderate resources had proved very popular running into several editions. Another publishing firm well established and one of the leading in the country brought out a book on the same subject. It bore the same title, get-up and lay-out as the first but was written by an indifferent author, whose name appeared in such inconspicuous letters at one corner that it would have gone unnoticed. It was simple for anyone to take this book for the book by the authority. Copies of this volume appeared in all the stalls and the first publisher was distraught. He knew the layman would be taken in by the second publisher's fraud. But he had neither the money nor the resources to fight the case in court. At this stage, he thought he should seek astrological guidance.

In Chart 68, the Ascendant Virgo is occupied by Vargottama Ascendant lord Mercury. The 7th house ruling opponent (second publisher) is occupied by Vargottama retrograde Jupiter. The 7th house does seem stronger but for the aspect of Saturn, a malefic on the 7th lord. Since Mercury was in a cuspal degree, legal action was not advised. On the other hand, the Lagna Rasi enclosed on both sides by benefics Mercury and Venus suggested things would move to his advantage.

7-40 a.m. (IST) on 21-9-1975 at Bangalore.

Should we file a suit against publisher X for copyright infringement? (Chart 68)

Moon 11° 50'	Jupiter (R) 0° 27'	Ketu 2° 36' Mars 28° 19'	
	Chart 68 Rasi		Saturn 8° 17'
			Venus 3° 33'
	Rahu 2° 36'	Mercury 0° 41'	Sun 5° 25' Lagna 25° 55'

As such, it was suggested, the querent (first publisher) should write to the second publisher protesting on his unethical and unscrupulous fraud on the reading public. He was asked to wait after that and do nothing. There was not even an acknowledgement of the letter sent by the second publisher. However, a couple of months later, a new edition of the book was released by the second publisher with the title rewritten in such a manner that no one would take it for the other. What brought about this change in the second publisher is a riddle, but the astrological indications were proved right.